BULL IN THE RING

Surviving and Thriving in Middle Management

M. Shane Putman

Copyright © 2017 by M. Shane Putman

All rights reserved. No part of this publication may be reproduced, distributed or transmitted in any form or by any means, including photocopying, recording, or other electronic or mechanical methods, without the prior written permission of the author, except in the case of brief quotations embodied in critical reviews and certain other noncommercial uses permitted by copyright law. For permission requests, email the author at the address below.

author@shaneputman.com

Ordering Information:
Quantity sales. Special discounts are available on quantity purchases by corporations, associations, and others. For details, contact the author at the address above.

Bull in the Ring/ M. Shane Putman. —1st ed.
ISBN 978-1976122187

Dedicated to the memory of Dr. Jim Underwood—for his irreverence, his brilliance, and the many kindnesses shown to a graduate student who knew absolutely nothing.

Thank you to the many people making this endeavor possible. The encouragement of my literary publicist (and wife) Janene was critical to my beginning this endeavor.

The collaboration of Sgt. Tyler McLain and Capt. Robert Kirkwood provided management insights into U.S. military forces.

(All errors are my own.)

Contents

PREFACE 5

WHO ARE THESE PEOPLE? 9

THE "FAILURE" OF STRATEGY 20

DIAGNOSIS AND RECOVERY 28

DRIVE YOUR OWN DESTINY 44

RECOGNIZING OPPORTUNITIES 56

BUILDING YOUR IDEA PORTFOLIO 67

PUTTING IDEAS INTO ACTION 75

BRINGING IT ALL TOGETHER 81

FROM MIDDLE MANAGEMENT TO…WHAT? 98

CROSSING THE FINISH LINE 107

Preface

What is the purpose of this book? The purpose is to build a foundation upon which today's middle managers may best apply individual skills, experiences, and abilities to the critical role of mid-level management. This book does not provide a definitive 12-step guide to managerial success. This book does not give prescriptive models on how to manage people. This book does provide a mental model by which any individual may leverage their strengths, abilities, and experience to create the highest *potential* for success in demanding work environments.

Middle managers are truly "in the middle" of their organizations, with demands and pressures coming at them daily from bosses, employees, and peers. The middle management role is more complex, challenging, and frustrating than ever. However, with increasing demand and pressure comes greater opportunity. Middle managers move strategy from the executive offices to the streets. Middle managers transform ideas into daily operating plans for workgroups, departments, and divisions. Middle managers are not middle children—they should not feel left out or underappreciated.

Middle managers reading this book will have tools available to:
- translate organizational strategy into action plans
- determine key objectives for their teams and themselves

- implement strategic plans within their sphere of influence while meeting current business demands

Strategy is no longer solely the responsibility of the executive suite. The most effective organizational strategy is created with the knowledge and input of middle managers. Strategic plans highlight desired results. It is middle managers who determine "what to do and how to do it" for the organization to effectively implement any strategy. This is why middle managers are a critical asset of any organization—they clearly understand how everyday activities contribute to strategic objectives. That beginning-to-end understanding allows middle managers to make effective decisions when daily pressures and demands require extraordinary effort to survive (much less succeed). The most effective middle managers can run through the forest dodging trees, roots, and branches while keeping the entire forest in view.

I have been a university business instructor since the 1990s, but this book is not intended as an academic resource. This book is neither structured nor written for the classroom. This book is for those managers working day-in and day-out to meet the demands coming at them from every direction. There are millions of words published by experts with much higher IQs than mine detailing how to perform managerial tasks. This book does not illustrate how to perform the daily functions of a middle manager, but highlights how to *think* while reducing stress and providing direction with greater control over a managerial career.

One of my favorite methods of challenging students in presentations and proposals is this: can you explain your idea to anyone on the street, in less than thirty seconds, well enough to have a five-minute conversation about the topic? That level of familiarity allows management theory to move from the classroom to the cubicle. A quote attributed to Albert Einstein states, "If you can't explain it simply, you don't understand it well enough." This book is direct, straightforward, and most of all, to be applied in "real life".

I am too simple a thinker to write any other way.

"You've got to think about big things while you're doing small things, so that all the small things go in the right direction."

~Alvin Toffler, American Writer and Futurist

CHAPTER ONE

Who are These People?

*"The unreasonable man attempts to adapt the world to himself.
The reasonable man attempts to adapt himself to the world.
Therefore, all progress depends on the unreasonable man."*
~George Bernard Shaw, Irish Playwright

Who are middle managers? In the corporate world, middle managers are typically located below the third or fourth levels in the company's organizational chart and include all positions that oversee other managers. They have leadership responsibility for a mix of managers and direct reports. In function, middle managers are the bridge between strategy creation and strategy execution.

Why should we dedicate time, energy, and research to the role of these unsung laborers? Aside from the impact they provide through the employees and businesses they manage, middle managers are the single highest contributor to workplace culture, whether that culture is great, horrific, or astoundingly mediocre. Research published by Gallup, Inc., one of the world's most respected sources of business analytics and advice, shows that up to 70% of the variance between good and great cultures can be found in the knowledge, skills, and talent of team leaders. In other words, the quality and attractiveness of collective culture rests with frequently under-appreciated middle managers.

Middle managers' impact on culture is valid for all organizations, inside and outside of the business world. Within the ranks of America's military, the same conditions exist within their specific "middle management." For this book, we will consider the military's middle management as the E5-E8 (Sergeant through First or Master Sergeant) ranks of enlisted personnel, and the O-3 or O-4 (Captain and Major) ranks of officers. Throughout these chapters we will discuss specific topics and findings from various members of the U.S. armed forces. Why include military organizations? There are two good reasons to do so. First, study of today's military closely mirrors observation of the business world (both are made up of people, after all). Second, the ranking system of the military makes it very easy to identify those with mid-level management responsibilities so we can focus on their experiences.

Let us begin by addressing a common myth—strategy originates from executive-level management. Middle managers represent both executives and workers and bear the responsibility of hearing, interpreting, and translating messages up and down the entire corporate hierarchy. They support and implement the overall corporate strategy while empathizing with their workers' struggles. In short, middle managers transform strategy into daily reality by the simple method of:

- translating strategy into functional business plans
- directing employees
- "owning" their area of responsibility
- directing the daily activities of the largest segment of people

What is the impact of middle management for an organization? A typical organization of 50,000 employees will have 50 to 200 senior executives and approximately 7,000 middle managers overseeing the functions and performance of about 43,000 employees. In other words, middle managers directly influence over 80% of a typical company's total workforce every single workday. These managers are vital for long-term success.

Yesterday's World

In years past, a middle manager enjoyed significant respect as part of an organization, representing an investment of time and demonstrated success. While not glamorous, middle managers were the primary mechanism to manage frontline workers and align workers' actions with executive directives. In the mid-1980s, middle managers were threatened with a changing environment in which executives were to get back in touch with customers and employees. This time period was when we first heard the word "downsizing". Market pressures from foreign competitors and federal deregulation of entire industries resulted in large enterprises like General Motors, IBM, AT&T, Eastman Kodak, and

Mobil Oil being forced to focus on cost cutting and flattening the organization by eliminating layers of management between executives and frontline workers. Unfortunately, the ranks of middle managers were ready targets for increased workloads accompanied by wage and headcount reductions. By reducing the number of individuals in middle management, companies frequently lost valuable resources who possessed:

- extensive experience in the company
- consistent high performance
- tremendous knowledge of the organization, suppliers, and customers
- insights on how improvements could be made by knowing how things get done and by whom they're done

Unfortunately, the middle management role is frequently considered as merely a temporary stop on the journey to an executive position. Most large companies make little effort to retain the most effective middle managers and invest few resources into expressing appreciation for these managers' contributions. Managers have grown accustomed to this difficult environment, accepting they should do everything possible to shed the "middle" label and progress to a general or executive management position.

In the real world, productive middle managers are a valuable resource. When a truly effective middle manager is removed from their role, finding a comparable replacement is highly unlikely without investing a great deal of time and training. This value does not always translate into job security, however. Sadly, many companies considered to be high performers by Wall Street and public opinion emphasize an official or unofficial "up or out" policy with their more tenured employees. In these companies, if an employee is not considered promotable within the next 12-18 months, *regardless of how effectively they perform their current role*, pressure will be applied for the employee to embrace other opportunities. This policy is an absolute waste of talent and knowledge. Many managers enjoy managing in the middle—they like the variety, the pace of change, bringing structure to ambiguity, and helping others be successful. They know they are effective in those roles and contribute value to the organization. All organizations would do better to support the best of these managers, reward their contributions, and encourage them to stay in the middle, if that is their choice.

If your organization does not have these supporting programs, propose to help create and actively support a formal career path that does not necessarily involve promotion out of middle management. The method I favor most is crafting a skill inventory of the best middle managers and understanding the areas at what each individual excels. Suggest assignment to teams or units where these managers can use special talents in interesting, challenging ways to create or increase value. Does one of them excel at performance turnarounds? Is another gifted in creating a supportive and collaborative team environment? How about those skilled at resurrecting supposedly doomed projects? If no program of this nature currently exists, build a proposal for it!

If you are a manager with a very specific, demonstrable and recognized skill of this nature, make sure that fact is known to your management. In addition, keep your eyes open to identify opportunities to leverage your skill outside of your immediate work group. There are many benefits to marketing your abilities outside your direct management chain. First, it broadens your advancement or transition opportunities when you are ready to move from your current position. Secondly, it serves as a layer of protection for your continued employment by lending more widespread credibility to your personal value as an employee. This value enhancement can be critical when reductions in force are considered. The decisions for who is laid off and who is kept are made or greatly influenced by managers external to the affected departments or divisions.

The 1980s also saw an unprecedented rise in competitive pressures affecting American companies. Globalization, technology, and foreign competitors required companies to recognize and adapt to changing business conditions faster than ever before. For most organizations, the demand for change began greatly outpacing their ability to adapt. H. Igor Ansoff, a mathematician and business manager known as the Father of Strategic Management, referred to the rate and scope of change as "environmental turbulence". In other words, how fast were changes happening and how big were impacts resulting from those changes? Before the 1980s and early 1990s, most American companies were structured and managed to respond to a moderate rate of change. If we illustrated change on a scale range of 1 to 5, most organizations were firmly encamped at a level 3. At this level of turbulence, companies could readily adapt to changes demanded by their environment, because their capacity to adapt equaled the environmental demand to change. However, as competitive pressure and other environmental demands increased, so did the overall change pressures on companies, their strategies, and their middle managers, as illustrated in Figure 1-1.

Figure 1-1

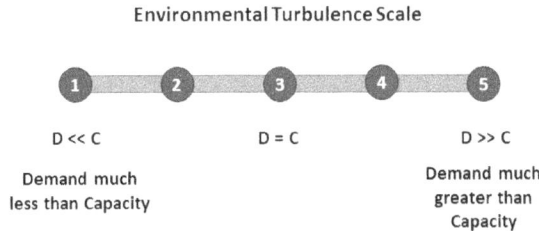

Today's World

Today, the industries of technology, healthcare, consumer manufacturing, and even government are required to meet the demands of turbulence well above Level 4 and approaching Level 5 in some cases. *All* industries are becoming more turbulent and many organizations are not able to change as quickly as their environment demands with traditional business practices. Decisions must be made more quickly by managers closer to the customer. As a result, the role of middle managers has expanded to include previously little-considered skill demands. Managers are required to develop a broader, longer-term perspective of their roles, responsibilities, and people-management requirements. Managers at all levels began to acquire or expand new skills and abilities to meet these challenges and fulfill these roles.

The Inevitable Result–Strategic Gap

When completing a strategic analysis of a global technology system integrator a few years ago, my research noted a recurring "strategic gap" between executive leadership, middle managers, and frontline employees. I have since worked for several global companies and consulted with many more, but the same circumstance exists with startling frequency. Many companies have solid strategies and highly capable front-line employees to perform the duties required by those strategies, but a great deal of confusion, misinformation, and reduced effectiveness exists within the middle layers of the organization.

Many companies provide extensive (and expensive) training programs to create sterling products and services for customers, retain employees, and generate revenue. I continually encounter front-line employees and first-line managers who fully grasp the "what" and "how" of their individual job requirements. However, these same individuals frequently demonstrated a basic lack of understanding how their job functions supported the overall strategy of the organization. Many middle managers remain unable to articulate exactly how their team translates corporate strategy into specific goals and objectives for individual group members. In most cases, this is no fault of the managers themselves as most managers are promoted from non-supervisory roles and have had little or no managerial training before accepting their new position.

Why does this blurring of strategy within the middle levels of an organization occur with such alarming regularity? Variance from strategy (or strategic drift), occurs from the daily pressures of management moving beyond their training or resources. Simply put, middle managers must:

1. demonstrate comprehensive understanding of strategy and direction inherited from levels above
2. work within the limitations of staffing, resources, and time
3. balance the inevitable conflicting goals and objectives directing the peer groups within their organization

No problem, right?

The World of the Middle Manager, aka "Bull in the Ring"

When I ponder the work demands of today's middle managers, I am reminded of my days playing high school football in Texas. At the risk of alienating some readers, I will use an analogy based on a team drill our coach loved to run with us.

Our benevolent head coach called the drill "bull in the ring." To begin the drill, the entire team would arrange themselves into a circle as illustrated below, with one fortunate soul chosen to be "the bull." (I choose not to dwell upon how many times I occupied this place of honor.) Players would then number themselves off in order, and for the duration of the drill, the assigned number would refer to each player.

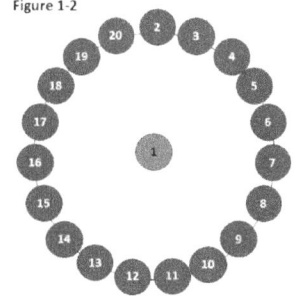
Figure 1-2

The purpose of the drill was simple: if you were on the perimeter of the circle (a "bull") and the coach called your number, you were to attempt to tackle, knock down, or otherwise physically discomfort the person in the middle to the best of your ability, then take up another position on the circle's edge.

Our coach would call random numbers one at a time and action would commence. In the beginning, it was a fairly easy drill–each person was numbered in order and the "matador" could anticipate which direction from which they would be attacked. However, as time progressed, the positioning of the "bulls" would become random, and the "matador" would have no idea from which direction imminent bodily harm would originate. (See illustration below). The environment changed. It became more complex, seemingly random, and frankly, more threatening!

Of course, our coach needed greater entertainment as the drill progressed, so he would begin calling out numbers in multiples– "3! 10! 18! 2!" At this point, the "matador's" head and body was in constant motion, scanning all sides, and reacting instantly to any perceived threat to his position (and overall physical health).

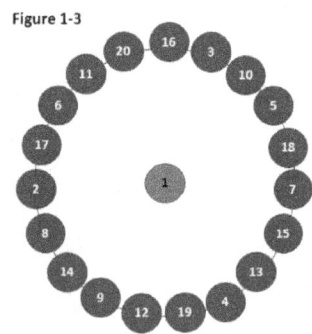

Figure 1-3

Welcome to the world of the middle manager! As with the "bull in the ring," demands are coming at middle managers from every direction. Each day, middle managers react to the latest "Monday Morning Memo" from executives, the current personal crisis from an employee, the most recent customer escalation, or the everyday demands of managing their group's responsibilities and meeting their performance scorecard targets. This executive ambiguity has been highlighted as an ongoing issue in military organizations as well. Significantly reduced troop morale results from frequently changing directives, with those in the lowest ranks suffering the most as they attempt to adjust their objectives and activities to an ever-changing landscape with little practical direction.

As with the football drill discussed above, only by recognizing approaching change demands (charging teammate), understanding their impact (they're trying to hit you very hard), understanding the overall goal (learn to scan and recognize change in your environment), and responding accordingly (deflect impact, stay on your feet, and be prepared for the next challenge) may middle managers not only survive, but thrive in today's turbulent organizational environments. When managers understand overall strategy, recognize change triggers, and implement a response plan for their teams, they retain a much greater control of their own destiny.

In Summary

Middle managers are the pipeline between the executive team and the rest of the organization.

The 1980s saw the perceived value of the middle manager reduced while workloads increased due to downsizing and corporate restructuring—an unfortunate trend that continues today.

Rising environmental turbulence requires an increasingly strategic mindset from middle managers.

CHAPTER TWO

The "Failure" of Strategy

"Failure is the opportunity to begin again more intelligently."
~Henry Ford, Automobile Manufacturer

Defining Strategy

Let's talk about strategy as a concept. Exactly what is "strategy?" According to the Merriam-Webster Dictionary, strategy is "a careful plan or method for achieving a particular goal, usually over a long period of time." A strategy is knowing where you want to go, where you are starting from, and what objectives are necessary to attain those goals.

Now we will move perilously close to becoming "academic." It is very difficult to talk about strategy as a separate concept from strategic planning. Strategic planning is the move from "why" and "what" of organizational direction to "how" to execute the plan. Libraries of literature exist on strategic planning. Consuming existing writings on strategy would require a lifetime and another lifetime to understand.

Now, what is *not* strategic planning? A common view of strategic planning is equivalent to financial management. For example, a quick online search found this definition at JobDescriptions.net: "A strategic planner is responsible for guiding the company through financial obstacles and helping to achieve its goal of continued profitability and growing revenue." While

awareness and knowledge of financial scenarios is certainly a key asset for all managers, it should by no means encompass the entire role. Successful strategic planning typically involves a group of people possessing the skills, experiences, and abilities to build solid links in the entire strategic planning chain—why, what, and how.

There is nothing complicated about strategy or strategic planning when viewed in its purest form. The complicated part of strategy is when people are added to the process. When people become involved, it becomes messy, illogical, emotional, and saturated with those behaviors that turn strategy and strategic planning from a science to ill-defined, free-form abstract art. However, successful strategy is *all* about the people.

When Strategy Goes Bad

In the early 2000s, Hewlett-Packard (HP) illustrated a fantastic example of middle management complexity. HP is one of the widest-ranging technology companies in the world with offerings from digital cameras to printers, IT systems integration, management consulting, and supercomputers. In 2002, then-CEO Carly Fiorina spearheaded the movement to acquire Compaq, a rival computer maker. Carly Fiorina's vision seemed sound: utilize the agility, engineering capability and customer base of Compaq to bolster and enhance the already impressive global reach and capabilities of HP. Many major stockholders bitterly opposed the acquisition, including Walter Hewlett. The merger did not go well in the following years, and Ms. Fiorina and HP parted ways in 2005.

During those years, I was affiliated with Microsoft Corporation's Partner Services division. Before the 2002 merger between HP and Compaq, Microsoft had large services contracts with both enterprises and continued to work with both throughout the merger. While my view into the organization was primarily in their services divisions, the difficulties of the merger were painfully obvious.

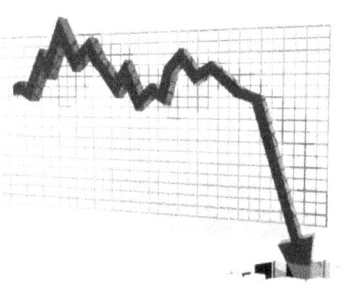

It was difficult for HP executives to grasp the complementary competencies of each company in addition to their cultural differences. From observation and later research, it appeared most of the failure could be traced to lack of trust and support among the key strategic relationships within HP—the board members themselves, some members of the board and Fiorina, the employees and the company, the shareholders and the board, and the shareholders and Fiorina.

Fiorina never secured the loyalty of employees, especially among the middle management ranks. *Business Week* published an article on February 25, 2005 stating Fiorina broke three key rules that CEO's must follow:

- place the company's well-being above all else, including yourself
- know your company from the inside out
- hold everyone accountable for results, including yourself

How did this situation present itself to middle managers within the company? To start, even as late as 2006, employees of the merged HP/Compaq companies referred to themselves and others as "HP Red" (former Compaq employees) and "HP Blue" (pre-merger HP employees). There was distrust between the groups based on disparaging perceptions of each other. Former Compaq employees perceived HP as trying to "drown" the Compaq culture. My contacts within the HP Red faction  viewed HP leadership in the same fashion as the Borg, a fictional alien race in the *Star Trek Next Generation* television series. The communications offered by the Borg to all other races consisted almost exclusively of these words: "You will be assimilated, resistance is futile." In like fashion, HP Blue employees seemed to view the former Compaq employees as rambunctious teens just entering adulthood, including a perceived air of "Welcome to HP! Let us show you how a REAL company operates."

Once the trust has been broken within any corporate, non-profit or military organization, these results will present themselves over time:

1. Leaders will recognize the situation and take proactive positive action to rebuild employees' trust
2. Affected employees will withdraw into only fulfilling their job descriptions to protect themselves as a career strategy
3. Wait for the next leader to rotate in, hoping for improved circumstances and an opportunity to contribute in a safer environment

Contributors to Strategic Failure

How is strategic disconnect created? At no time do the employees of a company meet in a break room, open their packed lunches, and collaborate to sabotage their company's strategy. Most of the time, strategic drift is slow, difficult to detect, and in some cases, unavoidable. Strategic failure occurs every day in companies where every middle manager is dedicated to doing the right things to the best of their ability.

Strategic planning often fails for a variety of reasons, but in the realm of middle management, the key contributors to strategic failures typically fall within these categories:

- failure to understand the culture of the organization (especially outside of an individual division or group)
- failure to adequately execute strategic plans

- failure to function as a team at the executive level or other levels
- failure to develop values and culture to support the established strategy
- failure to do what is needed in a timely fashion
- failure to trust and support each other at the various levels of the organization
- failure to proactively prevent ethical and legal problems

These may seem to be separate contributing factors, but each of these "failures" is frequently created when an organization begins to pursue opportunities and make investments in initiatives and activities that are not directly aligned with the overall strategic direction.

Every organization consists of multiple work streams focused on attaining a set of established objectives. Each workgroup exists to support the organizational strategic objectives as outlined by the organization's key decision makers. In a perfect world, all workgroups within an organization are aligned with the overall strategy and a common cause.

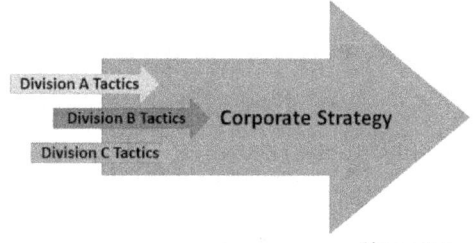

Figure 2-1

Figure 2-1 illustrates appropriate workgroup integration. In this instance, each subunit within the organization fully aligns with the corporate strategy and contributes directly to attaining those strategic objectives.

Now let's venture into the realm of harsh reality. Those individuals known collectively as "CxOs" – CEO, COO, CFO, etc., publish the infamous Monday Morning Memo outlining the latest and greatest direction for the organization. Executives build these strategies around major forces affecting the enterprise as a whole, such as profitability, market penetration, market development, etc. Often, these strategies derive from middle management input and idea submissions, but many times these announcements are a surprise to those below executive ranks. In any case, middle managers are responsible for interpreting how those strategic directives are broken down into tactical business plans for individual workgroups.

As the overall strategy sifts downward through the organizational chart, each middle manager structures an implementation plan based on their group's goals, objectives, and performance criteria. (Otherwise known around the water cooler as "what we get paid, recognized, and awarded for.") Inevitably, each manager will have a somewhat differing interpretation of the new marching orders. Each small difference has little impact, but when added together, those slight deviations become wildly divergent goals and objectives for individual groups, as shown in Figure 2-2.

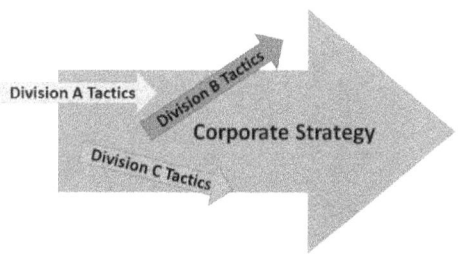

Figure 2-2

The top-level executive strategy is the most concrete and will undergo the fewest changes. However, as time progresses and each subunit follows their individual functional business plans, managers must account for the impact of changing business conditions. Changes in the competitive landscape, market influences, regulations, and other external forces will require modification of even the best business plans.

A certain level of misalignment is expected (and frequently desired) as groups adjust to take advantage of new opportunities and business demands. However, with each variance from the corporate strategy, there is a lessening of overall efficiency. Every organization has a limited supply of people, time, money, and opportunity, and any resource expenditure not in direct support of organizational objectives may reduce the overall return from those investments. This does not mean that these opportunities should not be pursued, but they should be pursued only after careful consideration and understanding of how those changes impact the overall strategy.

In Summary

 There are many contributors to strategic failure; all influenced positively and negatively from middle management levels.

 Strategic drift results in increasing conflict between workgroups and lessened return from resource investments.

 A certain level of strategic misalignment is expected and desired to take advantage of new opportunities.

CHAPTER THREE

DIAGNOSIS AND RECOVERY

"We can often do more for other men by trying to correct our own faults than by trying to correct theirs."
~Francois Fenelon, French Theologian, Poet and Writer

As time progresses, each group moves further apart and conflicts in individual business units become more visible and impactful. Most friction between workgroups arises from four primary causes:

- conflicting goals and objectives
- limited shared resources
- communication issues
- personality differences

What is the impact of these circumstances? Literature published by the University of Colorado estimates that up to 25% of a manager's time is spent resolving conflict. While I believe a certain amount of creative conflict is beneficial to an organization, there may exist better use of the leader/manager's time to increase productivity and a build a happier workplace.

Conflicting Goals and Objectives

Here is a simple scenario to illustrate this common theme. I have a relative who is branch manager of a well-known American bank. Imagine the world of a bank teller whose immediate boss  provides constant emphasis on prompt service and features that goal on all employee appraisals, recognition, and awards. A new regional community relations manager circulates a new email declaring that quality customer service is the highest priority for all employees. It will be a very short time before the tensions rise among all parties as speed is sacrificed to enhance a higher quality overall customer experience.

Conflicting goals and objectives are not always present when a corporate strategy launches–these circumstances develop over time as each business unit begins altering their individual tactics in response to changing conditions. Customer needs, regulatory changes, competitive pressures, and many other circumstances all contribute to these slight alterations in direction. These changes may seem insignificant when viewed individually, but during any typical workweek, a single small workgroup makes hundreds of these types of daily decisions. With that scale, small differences can quickly become huge gaps.

Limited Shared Resources

This subject does not require a lot of description. The budget for every organization is a finite resource for a limited number of items. Team managers do not typically attain their position without demonstrating a passion and belief in the team's mission, goals, and objectives, along with a willingness to be creative in attaining those objectives. A bigger slice of the pie for one team means less resources for another team, and very few managers will meekly allow the removal of resources without very clear reason and probably a direct order from their bosses.

Communication Issues

In my notes for this book, I originally had this item listed first, as communication (or the failure to communicate) is becoming a more divisive force in our companies. With the massive proliferation of email, social media, and self-produced video, one

would think these types of issues would decline. Unfortunately, many managers have become desensitized to the massive amounts of data and messages being thrown at them each day. In the managers' defense, trying to fully review, comprehend and respond to every request for their attention would rapidly result in a negative impact on all work. As discussed earlier, time is the most finite of all resources for a middle manager.

Unfortunately, transforming data into usable information may become a full-time job within itself for many managers.

I have one key piece of advice for communication: make sure every team member understands that effective communication is a *shared* responsibility between all parties involved. I have heard from multiple sources of the difficulty many managers have communicating with those team members classified as "millennials," or those typically born in the 1980s, 1990s, and early 2000s. Managers often receive negative feedback from this younger work force around communication difficulties—specifically, the manager doesn't understand how to connect with younger team members. I have no doubt communication problems exist in these situations, but these issues do not arise only from the manager's inability to convey ideas and instructions effectively. The skill of *listening* effectively must be built and exercised by the entire team.

> Effective communication is a shared responsibility.

During any communication, the sender not only has the responsibility to share information, but the sender has a responsibility to ensure the receiver has heard and understood the message. Likewise, the receiver has the responsibility to ensure they have heard and understand the message as intended by the sender. If there is a miscommunication between sender and receiver, the fault lies with both parties equally. In cases of obvious miscommunication, the sender and receiver should work together to understand exactly how the disconnect occurred as a learning opportunity to prevent such incidents happening in the future. The greatest benefit of listening is that it works with all people, regardless of age, gender, or ethnicity.

Personality Differences

This may be the most unavoidable of all conflict contributors. Thankfully, it is also one of the most easily addressed. Many personality evaluation tools are available, from the well-known Meyers-Briggs Type Indicator (MBTI) to some more modern and fun evaluators like the Schein Career Anchor evaluator, the Hearts, Smarts, Guts and Luck (Entrepreneurial Aptitude Test and *New York Times* bestseller), or the DiSC profile tool. Each of these models takes a differing approach and presents results differently, so use judgment to determine which is most appropriate for your group. However, all provide insight into how people perceive and interact with their fellow human beings.

Many managers question the value of personality inventories, and the investment in cost and time may be difficult to justify, so why should managers spend the time and budget to understand their people's personality type? The knowledge gained by the employment of these interpersonal development tools may:

1. Help managers to know what motivates an individual, give clues to what a person loves to do and will do well— enables effective delegation
2. Predict how people will behave in certain situations such as when under stress, coping with change, and making important decisions

3. Tell a manager how individuals will work when left to their own devices or given freedom to manage their own time
4. Answer the mystery of why some people relate well with coworkers and why others just do not work well with each other

I encourage every manager to apply one of these personality profile models to themselves and their team. Merely raising your team's awareness of differences, potential areas of conflict, and communications methods to prevent conflict is of great value. In addition to creating that awareness, the team will have a common language by which to converse with each other and resolve conflicts if (okay, not if—when) they arise. The most successful people managers are those who understand the people working for them on a very intimate level, accept them without wanting to change them as a person, give them work that suits their personality and temperament, and develop their strengths into new areas that help the employees grow. Great managers allow people to use their unique personality features to flourish in the workplace and make a unique contribution to the business. In short, great managers understand "people science."

The Science of People

The science of people frequently determines a manager's overall success. However, many companies, including those who are perceived as most successful and progressive in their business practices, hire and promote managers who demonstrate a higher level of technical expertise than their peers with little or no determination of leadership aptitude prior to promotion or hiring.

One of the companies seen as most progressive in their labor practices is Google. Google has experienced some significant growing pains in recent years concerning workplace and personnel policies, but those negative experiences have galvanized the company to take a very hard look at how they manage their people and human resource policies. Google conducted an internal study where they gathered and analyzed managerial feedback consisting of over 10,000 performance reviews, surveys and award nominations. Their findings provide some scientific basis to what many have theorized for years—technical ability is the *least* important competence area that employees value in their managers.

When the statisticians at Google completed their analysis, they compiled a list of the "Eight Habits of Highly Effective Google Managers." Listed below are the qualities Google employees valued in their managers, listed in order of importance.

1. Be a good coach
2. Empower your team; don't micromanage
3. Express interest in employees' success and well-being
4. Be productive and results-oriented
5. Be a good communicator and listen to your team
6. Help your employees with career development
7. Have a clear vision and strategy for the team
8. Have key technical skills to advise the team

A great manager does not attain greatness by how well they can perform their employees' functions. A manager becomes great by creating and nurturing an environment where each team member is comfortable in their role, has an open and honest relationship with their manager, and knows exactly how to provide value through their contributions.

Staying "On Strategy"

When I am discussing potential business ideas with an employer or client companies, every new concept or proposal begins with a discussion of whether the proposed changes are "on strategy" or "off strategy." While making that determination can be difficult, it is often quite simple. Each proposal for action should answer these questions: "Does this move our business unit in line with our corporate strategy?" and "Does this idea maximize our money, equipment, people, and time?"

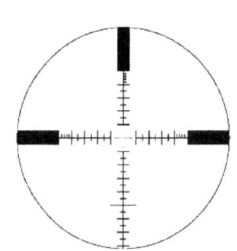

However, staying "on strategy" is more than making plans and making daily decisions in line with the unit mission or overall company strategy. A successful strategy establishes overall direction while allowing for modifications as changes demand. Leaders at all levels of the organization create, implement, and communicate strategy. Once the strategy is in motion, managers throughout the organization need to manage daily decisions to provide the results needed to bring that strategy to reality.

How do middle managers stay "on strategy" in the complete chaos that surrounds them every day? How do they even know what "on strategy" means? Depending on where you look, there may be hundreds of answers to these questions. There are thousands of articles, books, and training packages available on this topic. A significant number of these resources were created by experts in specific management areas and contain fantastic information. However, many of these resources are highly academic in style and content, making them difficult to understand on a practical basis and even more difficult to apply. The hundreds of managers I have interviewed and worked with have little time to read anything that may or may not be helpful. Today's managers have even less time to try to interpret highly academic research publications and writing styles.

I see three basic measures to judge the "strategic fit" of managerial decisions. These measures apply to any industry, company, geography, or culture with equal success. These measures are maximizing resources, maximizing capability, and maximizing investment return.

Maximizing Resources

Does the proposed action fully utilize my resources? Do the current people, structure, and processes support my proposal? How much will I have to redirect, change, or create to make it happen? Too often managers pursue ideas and opportunities that do not directly relate to the unit's mission or overall strategy. The result is a diluting of company resources away from maximum return, and contributing to the strategic gap we discussed earlier.

No business decision should ever be implemented without consideration of the overall strategic objectives, regardless of how attractive the immediate opportunity may seem. Within certain branches of the U.S. military, those who pursue individual initiatives not aligned with unit objectives are referred to as "good idea fairies" who flit around sprinkling shiny "fairy dust" on those around, providing distraction without contributing much of consequence. These people are viewed as personal glory chasers and not regarded highly within their units. In the corporate world as well, when a manager is perceived to be creating initiatives merely to increase their individual visibility, their personal credibility is greatly diminished in the eyes of peers and other managers.

Maximizing Capability

Does the proposed action strengthen the unit's "capability portfolio?" Will this decision better equip employees to respond to changing business conditions? These questions may sound more difficult than they actually are. Each manager should have a clear idea of what skills their employees possess and how those abilities contribute to the purpose of the group. To use a fairly silly example, having an employee on your team who can identify market trends a year in advance of your competition is hugely valuable, while an employee with a great deal of experience, ability, and proven success in income tax evasion would contribute little to your team or your overall success as a middle manager.

Maximizing Investment Return

Does the proposed action create more value to the organization than the resulting "weight?" In other words, is the resulting benefit greater than the extra work created or time required to implement? Have I engaged my employees where their skills, experience, and personality will provide the greatest value?

I have seen many circumstances where a new process or program sounds great in the planning phase but negatively affects those who should benefit. In one instance, I was working with a client company who contracted technical support to corporate customers. To enhance their services, the senior leadership team greatly expanded the information their account managers collected and tracked when customers experienced high-severity technical issues. This was a manual process, as the tracking system used by the support staff who solved customer problems was not connected to the system used by account managers. Each account manager was to use this data to determine if the cause of the problem was from the technology, the customer process, or a training issue and recommend appropriate services or actions to prevent future problems. This new process was expected to reduce the number of problems experienced by the customers, create additional revenue from new services sold, and increase customer satisfaction with the technologies overall.

The system changes were quickly announced and instructions sent to all account managers. This company had approximately 1,200 of these account managers and hundreds of these types of issues each week, so the investment of time and effort into this new initiative was quite significant. The flaw in the new process soon appeared. There was no method to report on any part of the new process. There was no way to know if the account managers recorded incidents. There was no tracking capability to determine if recommendations were made to customers. Finally, no means existed to determine if any recommendations made were accepted and implemented by the customers. Without this monitoring and tracking capability, no method existed to determine if the new process provided the intended value or was even followed! In this case, the new process created much more cost than benefit.

However, managers can avoid this trap by applying this simple model to business processes and group activities. When evaluating an existing or potential new process, assign that process one of three designations – CVA, BVA, or NVA. CVA is "customer value added", or an activity that the end user or *customer* would agree is beneficial and worth investing either time (for internal stakeholders) or money (for external customers). BVA is "business value added," or a process that enables the *organization* to perform basic value functions more efficiently or effectively. Activities that fit into the BVA category typically include collecting data for executive reporting, data protection initiatives to secure customer privacy, or other activities that do not create direct strategic value, but are still necessary. NVA is what we hope not to see— "non-value added," or those activities that have little or no tangible contribution to key activities. This simple method enables each work activity to be judged fairly and consistently. Processes that do not provide enough value for the resources used can easily be identified and altered or stopped.

Tools for Staying "On Strategy"

An extremely flexible and potentially powerful tool for evaluating these types of decisions is the Boston Consulting Group (BCG) Matrix, also referred to as the Boston Growth Matrix or BCG Matrix. The Boston Consulting Group introduced this decision support tool in the 1970's. The original tool used Future Attractiveness and Market Share as the primary comparison points, but I added "Experience" as well to encompass potential non-business decision scenarios in Figure 3-1.

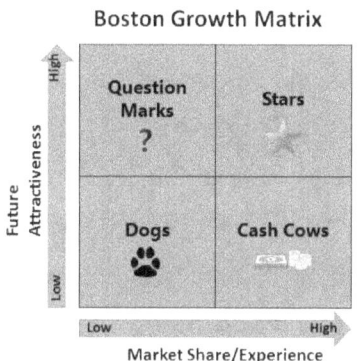

Figure 3-1

These matrix diagrams typically divide into four types of scenarios: Question Marks, Stars, Cash Cows, and Dogs. A user of this model takes any set of criteria (products, service lines, organizational divisions, key employees, etc.) and positions them in the appropriate quadrant at the appropriate level.

Question Marks: These parts of a business have high growth prospects but a low future attractiveness. They consume a lot of cash but bring little in return. In the end, Question Marks, also known as problem children, lose money. However, since these business units are growing rapidly, they do have the potential to turn into Stars. Companies are advised to invest in Question Marks if the product has potential for growth, or to discontinue if it does not.

Stars: These are business units or products with a great outlook for the future and which generate the most cash or overall benefit. However, a Star's high growth rate may consume large amounts of resources, as they require steady investment to promote continuous or increased growth. This generally results in the same amount of money coming in that is going out. Stars can eventually become Cash Cows if they sustain their success until a time when the market growth rate matures or declines and less resources are needed to capture market share or generate revenue. Managers and leaders most frequently invest in Stars to move their position into the Cash Cow quadrant.

Cash Cows: Cash Cows are marketplace leaders and generate more cash than they consume. These are units, products or activities with high market share, but low future growth prospects. Cash Cows often provide the investment resources required to turn Question Marks into market leaders. The revenue generated by Cash Cows is used to cover the administrative costs of the company, to fund research and development, to service corporate debt, make needed purchases, and to pay dividends to shareholders. Companies are advised to invest in Cash Cows to maintain the current level of productivity, or to "milk" the gains passively and fund investments elsewhere.

Dogs: Also known as "Pets," Dogs are units, products or activities that have both a low market share and a low growth rate. They frequently break even, neither earning nor consuming a great deal of cash. Dogs are generally considered cash traps because businesses have money tied up in them, even though they are bringing back basically nothing in return. Since Dogs have limited future attractiveness and will never generate more value, these business units are prime candidates for ceasing activities. If the Dogs are not delivering the cash to create profit or invest elsewhere, it is best to cut losses, discontinue those activities, and move those investments to areas of higher potential benefit.

What makes this approach helpful is its flexibility. You may substitute whatever decision criteria you desire. If you are evaluating specific team skills to emphasize in your next employee hire, you can replace Future Attractiveness with Upcoming Demand and replace Experience/Ability with Current Capability Level. In this scenario, your decision matrix may look like Figure 3-2. The difficulty in this exercise lies in making honest, truthful evaluations about the value of those comparison items in which you have a lot of experience, skill, or other market share. As illustrated with the Income Tax Evasion example, a high level of competency in any area does not necessarily indicate value. This model may also be easily applied to personal decision making. For example, if you're considering continuing your academic education in some form, you can evaluate the potential investment of time and resources in relation to other potential choices (family vacation, children's college fund, new car, etc.)

Figure 3-2

In Summary

 Each proposal should maximize your available resources, group capabilities, and investment return.

 The greatest potential value of middle management is ensuring day-to-day decisions support the objectives of the workgroup and organization–staying on strategy.

 Be careful of pet projects—just because something is done well does not mean it has value.

CHAPTER FOUR

DRIVE YOUR OWN DESTINY

"Man has been endowed with reason, with the power to create, so that he can add to what he's been given."
~Anton Chekhov, Russian Dramatist and Writer

IN today's world, many middle managers will manage scorecards perfectly, get solid evaluations, fulfill every aspect of their job description, and be passed over repeatedly for promotion and advancement. The managers (and individual contributors for that matter) receiving advancement opportunities have one thing in common – they drive their own destiny regardless of past or current circumstance. Each one evaluates their environment, determines triggers for change, and implements a plan to take full advantage of opportunity.

Managerial Balance

Turbulence is the perfect term to reference today's middle management environment. As the scope and impact of demands on organizations increase, so does the requirement for managerial decision speed and agility. In their book, *The Middle Manager*, Stephen Stumpf and Thomas Mullen present this as a "capability evolution" where middle managers must balance Efficiency (doing things right) with Effectiveness (doing the right things), and Embracing Change.

This balance is illustrated with a triangle positioned on a single point as reproduced in Figure 4-1. The emphasis of this illustration is any imbalance in the points of the triangle would result in the balance tipping and coming to rest on a flat side. This resting position may be comfortable and familiar to a manager, but could ultimately prove fatal to a career if allowed to persist.

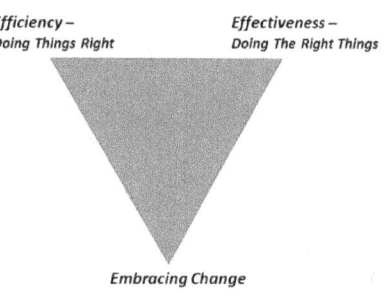

Figure 4-1

This triangle model is a valid illustration of the late-1980s and early-1990s business environment. This balancing act is a familiar dance to today's middle managers. However, as global competition, regulatory overhead, and technological advancements create an increasingly turbulent environment for all industries, I believe an updated illustration may more accurately reflect today's world.

First, embracing change may be a sufficient capability is a valuable asset for managers in modern organizations. Adaptability and willingness to change are desirable for all employees and much more desirable for "bull in the ring" middle managers. The most popular example of adaptive behavior and embracing change is discussed in the book *Who Moved My Cheese?* written by Spencer Johnson, M.D. The book was published in 1998, yet retains its original best-seller status as one of the most popular business publications ever written. Amazon describes the book with these words:

> *The message of "Who Moved My Cheese?" is that all can come to see it as a blessing, if they understand the nature of cheese and the role it plays in their lives. "Who Moved My Cheese?" is a parable that takes place in a maze. Four beings live in that maze: Sniff and Scurry are mice—non-analytical and non-judgmental, they just want cheese and are willing to do whatever it takes to get it. Hem and Haw are "little people," mouse-size humans who have an entirely different relationship with cheese. It is not just sustenance to them; it is their self-image. Their lives and belief systems are built around the cheese they've found. Most of us reading the story will see the cheese as something related to our livelihoods--our jobs, our career paths, the industries we work in--although it can stand for anything, from health to relationships. The point of the story is that we have to be alert to changes in the cheese, and be prepared to go running off in search of new sources of cheese when the cheese we have runs out.*

We cannot argue against the book's success as illustrated by the millions of copies printed and sold. However, I would expand the concept from merely change adaptation to change *creation*. The more successful middle manager of tomorrow will create opportunities to innovate, seek risk, create opportunity, and influence the future.

The triangle model portrays more stability and less turbulence than I see in today's corporate environments, however. I see more "motion" involved in balancing efficiency, effectiveness, and creating change. My favorite analogy uses a rapidly rotating wheel or fan, with each managerial demand making up one of the fan's blades as shown in Figure 4-2. As the wheel rotates, the fan blades maintain smooth rotation if each segment remains in balance with the others. When one blade becomes even slightly unbalanced, as long as the rotation remains slow, enough balance is maintained that the fan or wheel spins without the imbalance becoming destructive. When a blade or work area becomes unbalanced (as shown in Figure 4-3), the high spin rate demanded of today's middle managers produces instability. Over time, this uneven rotation will create significant damage to the overall mechanism. Suboptimal performance of

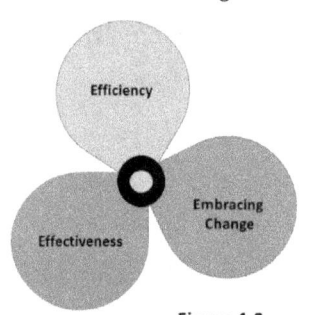

Figure 4-2

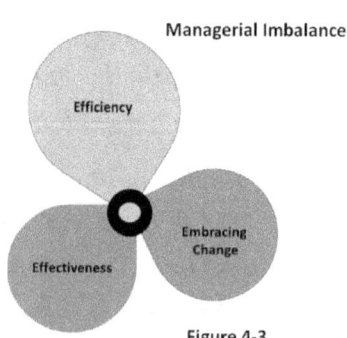

Figure 4-3

manager and team will be the inevitable result.

Creating change has become the driving force for all three segments of managerial balance. With industry and economic changes occurring with higher frequency resulting in increased impact on our organizations, the only way managers can ensure their efficiency and effectiveness is to judge how well their planning recognizes and effectively incorporates change.

Creating Change

Why the emphasis on creating change? Everyone understands that changes occur every day in all areas of our lives and we just deal with it–right? Unfortunately, that level of mental and emotional flexibility is uncommon by nature, but may be developed. I found many instances where middle managers seemed to be among those most resistant to change. My suspicion was supported when attending a change management certification course delivered by Prosci (http://www.prosci.com). We will explore the meaning and application of change management in Chapter 7, but we will review a few facts outlined in Prosci's research publication, *Best Practices in Change Management*, compiled from surveys and interviews with 822 change management practitioners in multiple industries around the world.

When investigating resistance to change, Prosci asked the participants how they identified resistance to change. The top responses were:

1. Observing behavior showing a lack of adoption or buy-in

2. Using feedback tools including readiness assessments, stakeholder analyses, email and social media
3. Seeking feedback through organizational channels and informal networks
4. Conducting meetings, interviews, focus groups and training workshops
5. Defining resistant behaviors and monitoring occurrences

The surveys then asked participants to identify the groups from whom they encountered the most resistance. Figure 4-4 illustrates the survey results. Surprise! The greatest reported resistance was – wait for it – *middle-level managers*. This clearly illustrates that many managers are not prepared to accept or embrace change much less create change.

Figure 4-4

There are many contributors to overall employee resistance, but the five key factors to managerial resistance are:
1. Lack of awareness—why are we making changes and what do the changes mean for me?

2. Impact on current role—perceived negative impact on job role or workload
3. Historical performance with change—past initiative failures, resistance from direct reports, etc.
4. Lack of visible support and commitment from higher-level management
5. Potential job loss

I would add another factor from personal experience. All managers have reached their current level of influence by their performance and achievements. Any proposed change asking these managers to behave differently from how they became successful will create a significant level of resistance. I encourage all readers to challenge themselves not to allow past successful behaviors to govern future decision-making. Change *will* occur around us. Whether we recognize or respond to it positively is purely our decision.

The implementation of any business plan that involves significant change must include intentional and prescriptive change management. Change management differs from project management in a very foundational manner – change management focuses on the people involved in the project in addition to the activities outlined in the project plan. Change management is not a substitute for project management, but complements and greatly increases the likelihood for project success by systematically and methodically managing how people understand and accept the change. We will discuss this in greater detail in Chapter 7 and review very actionable ways to incorporate the science of people into strategic planning and execution.

The Executive's World

In July of 2015, I hosted a conference session with Microsoft's Worldwide Chief Technical Officer, Norm Judah. One topic discussed in the session was how the executive decision-making process had changed over the past fifteen years or so. In years past, decisions passed down the organizational hierarchy, from top to bottom. Each level of the organization operated within their given parameters and the flow of information was relatively smooth and controlled. Granted, most communications were downward only from boss to employee, but the concept holds true. In our current global economy, the increasing speed of change around us has tremendously impacted how decisions are made by our top executives. Today's data aggregation and reporting capabilities are a two-edged sword. Executives spend a large amount of their time filtering through an ongoing tidal wave

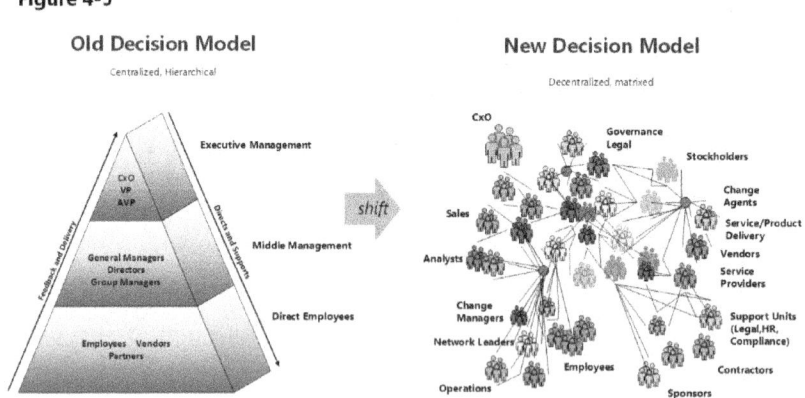

Figure 4-5

of information from nearly countless sources, as illustrated in Figure 4-5.

How about a broader example? In 2010, Booz & Company conducted a survey of more than 1,800 executives (including more than 480 top executive-level respondents) from companies of various sizes, from around the globe, and from a wide range of industries. The online survey asked twenty-one questions about strategy development, decision making, priority setting, capabilities, growth, and cost cutting. The findings were very interesting and are indicative of many, if not most, companies today.

> Linking priorities to decisions is a hurdle that few companies get past.

Executives in all industries indicated their companies lacked "coherence." These executives struggled with setting a clear strategy, ensuring that day-to-day decisions were in line with the strategy, and allocating resources to support the strategy. The research also showed companies with more coherence—where executives claim that strategy, capabilities and product offerings are coordinated—perform better. This struggle for strategic coherence is an issue not only for companies, but for individual executives as well. Survey respondents reported their biggest challenges were (a) ensuring that day-to-day decisions are in line with the strategy (56%) and (b) allocating resources in a way that really supports the strategy (56%). While most executives claimed their company had a clear direction to create value, most (53%) stated employees and customers did not fully understand this direction. Paul Leinwand, co-author of *The Essential Advantage*, verbalized the critical importance of linking strategy to daily decision-making perfectly in *How to Win with a Capabilities-Driven Strategy*:

> The survey results tell us that deciding on priorities is a huge issue for companies — and that actually linking priorities to decisions is a hurdle that few companies get past. We see this 'incoherent' operating environment across industries and geographies, among all types of companies. It is draining — and forcing companies to pay a significant penalty. We call it the incoherence penalty.

What does this mean in the context of our discussion? The complexity of the strategic decision process makes it nearly impossible for a single leadership team to devise, implement and monitor the alignment of all business activities, no matter how talented the team. In simpler terms, executive leaders are desperately seeking good ideas and actionable proposals, regardless of the source!

A basic truth of companies is this: The further you move down the organizational chart, the closer you come to your markets and customers. Those in your company who know the most about your customers are those who meet them face-to-face. This customer knowledge is where a middle manager has the greatest opportunity to transition from being an employee to becoming a strategic asset of the company.

> **Middle managers have the greatest opportunity to turn corporate strategy into reality.**

The opportunity described for middle managers is not merely the fevered delusion of my occasional chaotic thinking. In July 2010, the Boston Consulting Group (BCG) published an article entitled, "Creating a New Deal for Middle Managers." This article targets upper-level executives who are "empowering a neglected but critical group." The article's theme revolves around creating an environment for middle managers to excel. BCG's proposed change model encourages executives to determine if there are too many management layers in the current organization. The reasoning behind this evaluation is to seek opportunities to reduce the number of layers in the overall organization, create broader, more impactful roles for middle managers, and remove the artificial barriers that currently create frustration and stifle initiative. While implementing the BCG recommendations may mean fewer middle managers overall, those remaining will have more meaningful positions with tangible impact. Organizations may then invest more time, energy, and overall resources into producing results vs. administrative and coordination of activities. A significant responsibility of managers in these flattened organizations will be strategic thinking along with implementing strategic change initiatives.

This is a radical change of thinking for many managers who rose through the ranks to attain a management position. Managers were promoted by doing their jobs well, keeping customers happy, and meeting commitments. Creating a self-

> Those who cling to the past embrace the greatest risk.

imposed mandate to move "out of the box" and actively seek new thought processes, behaviors, and personal development may seem a huge transition with a great amount of personal risk. I respond to that feedback with this thought: The increasing speed of change means that those who cling to the past embrace the greatest risk. However, the greatest opportunities exist for those who actively seek new options, construct a plan to embrace those opportunities, and execute that plan effectively. The future is for those who balance efficiency, effectiveness, and create change.

In Summary

 Managers must balance efficiency (doing things right) with effectiveness (doing the right things) while embracing change and preparing for the future.

 Executive leaders do not have all the answers and are often desperately seeking knowledgeable input and ideas.

 Middle managers have the greatest opportunity to turn corporate strategy into reality.

CHAPTER FIVE

RECOGNIZING OPPORTUNITIES

"Everyone you will ever meet knows something you don't."
~Bill Nye (Science Guy)

Now we come to the most time-consuming activity in this book–recognizing opportunities to create change that is on strategy with the overall organization but can still be communicated and implemented on a team level. How does a manager who is new-to-role or unfamiliar with strategic decision-making find these opportunities to create change?

> Opportunities are never lost – someone will happily take the ones you miss.

This stage begins with information gathering on the strategies and direction of your overall organization or company. We will focus on sources from both publications and interpersonal relationships to gather this type of data. Of the five sources listed below, three are oriented toward internal information usually only available to employees, but two are from public sources readily available with a minimal amount of research. These information sources are:

1. Annual reports/SEC filings
2. Company slogans and corporate initiatives
3. Corporate initiatives
4. Skip-level one-on-one meetings
5. Multi-networking

Each of these provides a different perspective on strategic direction for any organization.

Annual Reports/SEC Filings

Annual reports are a fantastic source of information on a company's direction, even for veteran employees. This document is not merely a dry volume of financial data and statistics. An annual report is a summary of activities throughout the preceding year and a high-level view of future direction for the company. Annual reports give shareholders and other interested parties information about business activities and financial performance. In the United States, a more detailed version of the report, called a Form 10-K, is submitted annually to the U.S. Securities and Exchange Commission (SEC) by publicly owned and some privately owned companies.

These reports are typically found on the company's primary public website, in a section entitled "Investors" or something similar. The ease of reading these reports may vary widely, as the formats differ greatly and are dependent on industry standards and legal disclosure requirements. Regardless, an annual report contains most or all the following sections that may contain information relevant to a middle manager's data gathering efforts:

Letter from the Chairman

This section is typically executive "pep rally propaganda" for investors and analysts. Content typically highlights management performance and key data items such as corporate goals and high-level strategies for the future.

Sales and Marketing, or Business

Included here is a description of products/services with major divisions and groups and what they do. Information here includes the most important products, which divisions or groups are most critical to company's success, and identified risk factors. What are the company's environmental vulnerabilities? Do cyclical buyer activities impact anticipated revenue? What are the fixed-price revenue streams? Are there upcoming regulatory or contract compliance issues?

Summary of financial results

This section is a financial overview with anticipated trends in growth (or non-growth) of revenues, profit and other leading indicators of financial success.

Management discussion and analysis

Content encompasses open discussion of significant financial trends within the company over past years. Data in this section may include highlights of expected growth areas, potential cuts, and budgetary impact.

Financial statements

This is where a company exposes detailed financial performance data for all to see. Highlighted content includes organizational structure and financial items that have not been publicized elsewhere, e.g. management reorganization or write-offs.

Subsidiaries, brands, and addresses

This section outlines company locations and key contact information, brand names, and product lines along with potential sources of talent, internal performance benchmarking, and multi-networking opportunities.

Other included sections not typically relevant to our purposes are:

- **List of directors and officers**
- **Letter of CPA opinion**—CPA audit firm statement of any qualifications found with financial data
- **Stock price history**—History of stock prices and dividends showing upward and downward trends over time

Company Slogans and Corporate Initiatives

This may seem like a strange indicator of personal opportunity within either a corporate, non-profit, or military environment. After all, how do the words printed on the posters in the breakroom and over the water cooler aid in planning for your business unit? The straightforward answer is this–when a company invests the resources needed to establish a new slogan or advertising campaign (frequently costing millions of dollars), it indicates a serious desire to establish a change in direction, culture, or external perception of the company. Such initiatives represent big bets by the senior leadership team, both for the organization and their individual careers.

How to apply this information? Here is an example. Several years ago, I participated in a corporate initiative to change how account managers assessed, planned, proposed, and delivered services to large customers, including global business enterprises, governmental agencies and branches of the military. To generate support for the change program within individual regions and customer segments, I met with key individuals to review and assess strategic opportunities with strategic customers. One such occasion was a meeting with one of the most senior account managers in the entire company. We'll call this gentleman "John". John is an extremely talented services consultant and has managed highly strategic Fortune 50-level accounts, including Intel, Boeing, and Southwest Airlines. One of his accounts had an annual multi-million-dollar services renewal approaching, so we were discussing the customer's needs and his draft proposal to ensure we were creating the greatest value for the customer (and the most revenue for the company, as well.)

As we were going through the proposal and John answered the continual stream of questions I asked, I happened to notice five words printed in the top corner of each of his presentation slides. When I asked him about the phrase, he stated, "That's the new slogan [the customer] announced last month. It is everywhere around their offices—on posters, coffee cups, you name it." When I asked John, "Why are they making this change?" he responded that he didn't know. I immediately encouraged him to find out as much as he could about this new initiative. Which executives were driving the changes? What results were the customer targeting through these changes? If the customer was spending the time, effort, and money to land a campaign of that breadth throughout their company, there was a specific change of business and behavior the customer leadership team was looking for. It was the perfect opportunity to discover the driving forces behind the changes and target our assessments, proposals, and recommendations to the goals and objectives of the client. John's recommendations and proposal would then be positioned perfectly to receive favorable attention (and budget) from the customer's executives.

The same reasoning holds true for middle managers. When your company invests the time, effort and money in such a program, it is in the best interest of all involved to determine what the desired end results are and focus planning on how you and your group may directly support those objectives. Take the plan to your leadership team and verify your thoughts. At best, they will appreciate the effort to contribute and offer suggestions or more tangible support to help you implement your plans. At the very worst, you will be able to confirm your understanding of the key focus areas and make any adjustments necessary. Again, even if significant changes to your understanding and planning are needed, your management will understand your thought process and demonstrated desire to support their initiatives.

Skip-Level One-on-One Meetings

If you are not familiar with the term "skip-level," it refers to setting up one-on-one meetings with managers or executives further up the organizational chart than your direct manager. While this may seem intimidating and maybe even somewhat arrogant if you are not accustomed to them, these are a fantastic opportunity to ensure your current planning and implementation efforts are in line with the overall organization.

These meetings are not only able to confirm your understanding of the current plans and strategies of the organization, but allows opportunity to inquire about potential future company direction, what those changes could mean for your group, and brainstorm the most effective programs to directly contribute desired results.

Multi-Networking

This may be the most underutilized information gathering method of those listed here. Multi-networking is having relationships and information channels from multiple sources. This means having relationships with people throughout all levels of your organization, from the executive suites down to the cafeteria cashiers. Information is not a resource dedicated solely to corporate officers. Cleaning staff, cashiers, cafeteria workers, and IT staff see and hear items of interest not necessarily visible to official sources. These unconventional sources provide the potential for seeing organizational patterns and verifying information outside of "official" channels. A rumor or story shared in the breakroom may be easily verified or disproven with a few inquiries sent through a well-developed personal network.

Although competitive intelligence gathering may be automated to some extent with current data mining and machine learning technologies, it is still primarily a people-driven activity. It requires direct participation from people at all stages to work effectively. To achieve the highest potential success in your information-gathering efforts, you need to have the right mix of people with different personalities and views of the overall organization. Multi-networking is a great way to identify and clarify opportunities, because it exploits the strengths of the multiple organizational personalities illustrated in Everett M. Rogers' article titled, "The Diffusion of Innovations." These "Five Personalities of Change" highlight differing organizational personalities and the contributions from each:

Pathfinders are the first people to see change coming, yet represent only about 2.5% of the general population.

Listeners are receptive to what pathfinders say and have the organizational credibility to be heard by those in executive power. Listeners represent 13.5% of the population.

Organizers are the detail-oriented, driven personalities who most often become executives. They may be resistant to change, however, explaining why organizers frequently lead organizations to failure. Organizers comprise about 34% of the general population, but up to 80% of corporate CEOs fall into the Organizer category. Organizers typically have little access to Pathfinders, but may have access to their views through Listeners.

Followers will generally have nothing to do with Pathfinders and resist change, but they are tenacious. Assign them a task and they will get it done, even in the face of adversity. Followers are great in roles such as sales, because they can tolerate high levels of rejection. They contribute another 34% or so of the general population.

Diehards fill about 16% of organizational seats and may embody a near suicidal resistance to change. These people would be the charter members of the Flat Earth Society, if such a body existed today. Given the chance, they would probably shoot the pathfinders, but they are staunchly faithful to the organization.

A fully developed personal network includes people from each of these personality groups. Each personality type sees the same situation differently, and a combination of all provides a holistic view of the organization and existing opportunities.

Research performed by MIT Sloan School of Management professors Ralph Katz and Tom Allen supports the benefit of multi-network contributors. They studied research and development (R&D) teams to investigate the relationship between the length of time a team had been together and the level of communication between project groups. As measured by department managers and laboratory directors, the higher-performing groups had significantly more communications outside their immediate work teams, whether with other internal groups or outside contacts. In addition, groups who had been together the longest reported lower levels of external communications and "were significantly more isolated from external sources of new ideas." This seems very reasonable, as

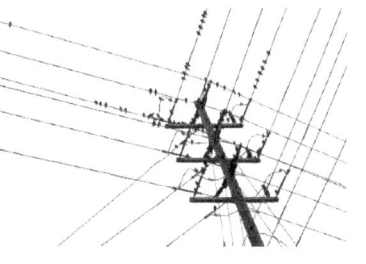

members of newer teams will retain a personal network outside of their current workgroup, while members of more longstanding teams have probably allowed their personal contacts with outside groups and organizations to erode and wither away.

Ideas are only as good as the information upon which they are based. Research and practical experience has shown that innovation arises from just about any source. IBM performed a global study of CEOs and concluded that two-thirds of the most significant sources of innovative input comes from outside the home organization. These unexpected sources of innovation may include customers, suppliers, partners, research and development divisions, etc. Deliberate development of multi-level network sources construct and communicate a more complete view of opportunity.

Today's managers should intentionally distribute the focus of attention between day-to-day operations and the unstructured, untried, and untested. A good manager has key people on their team trained and available to ensure daily operations occur effectively with minimal direct oversight. The practice of identifying and developing group leads is a time-proven practice that both gives and takes away—both in a positive way. First, having standard daily operations managed by key team members takes away managerial stress by dividing the workload of oversight among a group versus an individual. This structure allows the principle of "we are all together smarter than any one" to exist in everyday practice. Secondly, it gives time for innovative thinking, planning, and recognition of key opportunities to create and drive change. How to invest these time savings? Seek out and recognize opportunities to lead change rather than merely manage it.

In Summary

Follow the money—investments being made within your organization are key indicators of future focus and strategic emphasis.

Annual reports, (SEC) filings, company slogans and lunchroom posters are readily available sources of strategic information for many organizations.

Always keep in touch with your key customers, managers, and internal network. A seemingly trivial conversation with the manager of the building cafeteria can produce huge returns!

Reserve time and attention for innovation. Seek opportunities of calculated risk for the untried and untested.

CHAPTER SIX

BUILDING YOUR IDEA PORTFOLIO

"Don't worry about people stealing your ideas. If your ideas are any good, you'll have to ram them down people's throats."
~Howard Aiken, American Physicist and Computing Pioneer

Creating and driving change requires much more listening and communication than everyday job activities. With the huge amount of data available to today's executives, one of the most valuable contributions from middle managers consists of turning that data into meaningful information that is actionable and on strategy.

Leaders are those who seize opportunities as they are recognized while actively encouraging and coaching others to do the same. When I discuss projects with coworkers, clients, and friends, I have found that many personal victories were in circumstances where they were assigned a project, task, or mission without prior consultation or any right of refusal. Everyone can drive highly innovative changes within a project that was not self-created. Let's be honest: "stuff" happens. Sometimes that stuff exists from our own initiative, but it happens to us as well. Many business challenges arise from rapidly changing environmental conditions, and those changes demand effective leadership to address. If assigned an unexpected project, recognize it as an opportunity to demonstrate your personal flexibility and ability to deal with ambiguity.

Personal networking will yield great opportunity, but other personal activities contribute to potential innovation as well. Below are three primary mental models that contribute greatly to an innovative, creative mindset.

#1 Learn from Every Opportunity

An executive for a former client had a personal philosophy shared throughout his organization: It takes approximately two years to learn your job thoroughly. In his mind, if you have been in your position for less than twenty-four months, there was much to be learned in your current role and you were highly discouraged from seeking other opportunities. While I see how this policy could both benefit and hinder an organization, there is one thing that is true of any organization, corporate or military: the faster changes occur, the greater the negative impact from employee turnover. For example, one staff sergeant I interviewed spent part of his active duty stationed in Korea. The average duty length for those stationed there was only one year. This sergeant was an exceptionally forward-thinking individual with innovative ideas, but rapid turnover of personnel made it difficult to establish proven standard operating procedures and create a stable working environment. This instability contributed further to the high level of transition, creating a vicious cycle of continued inefficiency and slow progress.

When discussing the twenty-four-month policy with that executive's employees and direct reports, I found that longer-tenured employees implemented this guideline a bit differently. For those employees who had been in their position for longer than ten years (some much longer), their approach to job planning was, "If I was starting this job today, what would I do and how would I do it?"

This completely changed the viewpoint of several key employees. Their mindset changed from seeing their current job demands as a series of tasks to slog through into evaluating the impact their activities contributed and the value they created. These employees began managing each new assignment and announced change as a new beginning, or a "reboot" (to use technical terminology). They were alert for opportunities to improve their working environment from both operational and strategic viewpoints.

A very significant additional benefit materialized during this time of transition. Several former lower-performing, long-tenured employees within the division were re-energized and became much more productive. One of the best and easiest ways to transform lower-performing individuals and groups is to unlock their talent and resources by creating an opportunity to innovate and contribute. Challenge employees to do the same. Actively encourage them to identify and propose ideas they have nursed in the back of their minds and always wanted to implement. Even if the proposed idea is deemed off-strategy or not feasible for the current point in time, recognize the effort and drive shown by those who bring the ideas and reward efforts. Those employees will be more engaged in their daily activities and will remain vigilant for other opportunities to improve the environment for all.

#2 Ask "Why?"

This is the greatest weapon in the arsenal of any change agent, especially when introduced into a new workgroup or organization. Everyone expects the new person (or consultant) to ask simplistic (or silly) questions, so take advantage of the circumstance to ask "why?" at every opportunity. I'm continually amazed by how often the answer to such a simple question is "I'm not sure," "I don't know," or "That's just how we do things here." When I discussed this phenomenon with one of my military contacts, he responded, "We are doing the 'stuff' and the 'things'... but what exactly are we doing, and why are we doing it?" In digging deeper into the meaning of this statement, it was apparent that military "executives" (Sergeant Major, Lieutenant Colonel, and higher) are tempted to focus on the activity vs. demonstrated progress in their personal behavior and communications. As a result, these leaders' direct reports adopt similar behaviors until the overall organizational effectiveness is lowered. *Never confuse activity with progress.* Some of the busiest people I know accomplish the fewest results in terms of long-term value.

Standard practices, policies, and processes are critical to creating efficiency and maintaining productivity. I would never argue against efficiency gained from experience. However, many initiatives and processes are blindly inherited from the past, and have outlived the conditions where they provided value. There is a point where a single-minded drive for efficiency results in reduced effectiveness. Every manager should periodically evaluate his or her own reflection in these simple mirror questions:

1. What does my team do? (established practices, policies, and procedures)
2. Why are we doing it?
3. What are the outcomes of performing these actions?
4. Do these outcomes contribute to the overall strategy of our organization?
5. How do the outcomes contribute to our team strategy?
6. Are there other opportunities to contribute not in existence today?
7. Are there other actions or initiatives that would produce greater value?

While not always possible, try to perform this evaluation in conjunction with the entire team. Evaluate the findings for each item and assign each a value of "start," "stop," "change," or "remove." Part of the evaluation process is to identify those items that contribute to another group's activity or rely on contributions from another group. If your unit no longer requires that input, give the other group an unexpected gift and let them discontinue that activity. If another group no longer requires your process or output, give a gift to yourself and take back the resources and time allocated to that activity. Last step? Resolve to eliminate every needless rule, unproductive routine, and off-strategy activity you have identified.

> Eliminate every needless rule, unproductive routine and off-strategy activity.

You will be astounded at what you will find through the application of this simple evaluation. Here is a real-world example of the potential impact of this approach. I once led a team tasked with streamlining the job requirements of a key customer-facing role in a client company. A series of executive announcements had created new job requirements (and resistance) to the new role responsibilities. While the proposed changes directly supported a key market strategy for the company, employees in the targeted role felt completely buried under the weight of additional work demands given without clear priority guidance. My team's role was to streamline the list of activities currently required, establish priorities, and reduce the overall stresses on the affected employees.

To accomplish this lofty goal, we conducted focus groups to determine what tasks these employees were performing, prioritize the value created by those activities, and divest those activities either generating lowest value or even detracting value, in some cases. The team established recommendations targeting the removal or "alt-sourcing" (getting someone else to do) those activities that did not create value for either the client or their customers. When we completed our evaluations, the resulting change plan would reclaim thousands of work-hours per year for this single role, resulting in millions of dollars of productivity gained over time.

#3 Learn Your Boss's Job

Following my senior year in high school, I worked for a local entrepreneur, named Gary, to remodel and maintain the group of rental homes he owned in the area. Gary never had children of his own, but he poured wisdom into those who would listen if he believed they would pay attention. One fine 106^0 Texas summer day as I rested from replacing the roofing on his beloved racing pigeons' coop, he imparted this concise bit of wisdom: "Learn your boss's job." He explained his reasoning with two very simple principles that even a teenage boy could understand. "Knowing your boss's job results in two things – you are more valuable to your boss and your team and more promotable, and your boss is more promotable because a replacement is ready to assume the role when the boss moves on."

In Summary

Learn from every job and position.

Ask "why?" your organization or group does what it does. Most importantly, ask this of your role.

Be ruthless with those activities that do not support the mission or strategy. If it does not fit, eliminate it.

Learn your boss's job—this makes it much easier to promote both the boss and you.

CHAPTER SEVEN

PUTTING IDEAS INTO ACTION

"The only way to make sense out of change is to plunge into it, move with it, and join the dance."
~Alan Watts, British Philosopher, Writer and Speaker

The most critical aspect of any strategy, invention, or even a good idea in general is getting the concept into practice. Unfortunately, this is by far the most difficult phase to accomplish. Why is this the case? We have a clear idea of where we are, where we need to be to meet the demands of our changing future, and what it will take to embrace the needed changes. So why is there a problem putting ideas into action?

Let's go back to Chapter Two where we discussed how "When people become involved [with strategy], it becomes messy, illogical, emotional, and saturated with those organizational behaviors that turn strategy and strategic planning from a science into ill-defined, free-form abstract art." In my academic career as a business instructor, I have participated in multiple graduate-level programs that included studies of organizational behavior and organizational leadership. The one thing I have learned to be absolute truth is change occurs through the movement of individuals, **not** a mass migration to something new.

In the days of yesteryear when senior leaders ruled their kingdoms through strict adherence to bureaucracies and organizational charts, a "Monday morning memo" from a top executive would announce corporate changes with clear expectation that all employees in lower organizational levels would readily comply. Any resistance was typically managed by finding a scapegoat and making an example by public demotion, reassignment or outright release of an expendable employee, after which everyone else would fall in line. Today's employees have become accustomed to a higher degree of self-determination, personal engagement, and *much* greater workplace autonomy. This has long been true of the millions of white-collar information workers comprising our current workforce. However, increased job autonomy is rapidly becoming common among blue-collar

> Change occurs through movement of individuals, not a mass migration to something new.

industries as well, where the value of a skilled tradesman is higher than ever.

What does this mean for managers? Change is not something that is a "launch and forget" activity. Effective change demands intentional planning from creating announcements to behavior reinforcement and resistance. In its most simplistic form, organizational change is merely the conversion from a documented current state through the trials and tribulations of the transition period to reach a desired state, as illustrated in

Figure 7-1

Figure 7-1 below.

The process illustrated in Figure 6-1 is identical for every individual impacted by the proposed changes. Every affected person determines for himself or herself the expected impact upon the work environment for each change introduced. An effective manager never forgets that stresses introduced by change are cumulative. The stresses from each change initiative pile onto each other, frequently resulting in an overall employee stress level much greater than anticipated. To illustrate, here's a simple example. With a team of five employees, a change announcement will result in five different interpretations of how that change will affect each person. If we introduce another change to the same team, there will be the five original interpretations, five additional interpretations of the new change, and *five more* interpretations of how the changes together will impact each employee. In this example, one additional change results in up to fifteen opportunities for stress, confusion, and resistance to develop.

Each employee begins with their current state ("How do I do my job today?") and compares that baseline with their *perceived* future state ("How will I do my job after the change?"). I highlight "perceived" because each individual will estimate personal impact from the change differently as a result of assumptions, past experiences, and some guessing. Each person will then react to the expected change from his or her personal perception, whether in a positive or negative fashion.

This is the reasoning behind the emphasis on the people side of change management. On the positive side, implementing a defined framework of change within your organization or work group will:

1. Increase the probability of project success
2. Manage employee resistance to change proactively and effectively
3. Build and enhance the ability to change throughout the organization

In the same fashion, there are definite potential consequences for not addressing how individuals react and respond to environmental changes. Table 7-1 illustrates a sampling of these negative possibilities.

Table 7-1	
Lower productivity	Passive resistance
Active resistance	Employee turnover
Lower employee engagement	Use of process workarounds
Reverting to legacy processes	"Us" vs. "Them" mentality

The bottom line of change management is this—for change to be successful on both a short- and long-term basis, individuals must do their jobs differently. Change management methodologies like the one created by Prosci provide a framework for understanding how individuals change. Managers and project teams use these tools to guide change planning, diagnose root causes of resistance, and develop corrective actions in advance of encountering barriers.

While I will not attempt to give a complete overview of the Prosci change management methodology, a brief overview of their ADKAR© model is helpful for understanding how Prosci translates organizational change to an individual level. ADKAR is an acronym highlighting Prosci's five building blocks of successful change. These building blocks are:

> For a successful change initiative, individuals must do their jobs differently.

Awareness	Awareness of the need for change
Desire	Desire to participate in and support change
Knowledge	Knowledge of how to change
Ability	Ability to implement required skills/behaviors
Reinforcement	Reinforcement needed to sustain the change

The ADKAR principles are the foundation of the overall Prosci organizational change management process. The process documents and outlines in very practical detail their 3-Phase Change Management Process – Preparing for Change, Managing Change, and Reinforcing Change.

There are many change models available, however. The Prosci model is only one of these. I favor the Prosci approach for several reasons:

1. It is easy to comprehend and explain to others, even busy executives.
2. It is very practical in its documentation and approach and is not perceived as too "academic" for practical use.
3. It is a toolkit comprised of tools, templates and proven methods for planning, communicating, staffing and managing change efforts from "soup to nuts," or from idea to results.

The most important stage of any change program is not the planning, implementation, or even the launch and widespread rollout. The most important stage by far is *visible results*. Too many managers, executives, and organizations fall into the trap of confusing activity with progress. Unless the changes produce the value intended, there is no true success or even completion. A project is not complete when the final phase concludes and the new change launches. It is successful only when those affected can accomplish their goals easier, faster or more effectively as a result of the change.

In Summary

 Change does not occur through programs, change occurs through people.

 Understanding and planning for the impact of change upon differing groups of people and key individuals greatly increases potential for successful change.

 Ensure your change efforts create value and the desired outcomes. All else is a poor investment of time, effort, and people.

CHAPTER EIGHT

Bringing It All Together

"We are called to be architects of the future, not its victims."
~Buckminster Fuller, American Architect, Author, and Inventor

To summarize what we have discussed so far—we began with a review of who middle managers are and the value their knowledge and skills bring to their organizations. We next examined how important strategy is to managers of all levels and how uninformed tactical decisions introduce strategic drift. We reviewed the concept of driving our own destiny by recognizing opportunities as part of our everyday actions. We highlighted the benefits of building an idea portfolio and discussed how we implement those ideas. Now, we will compile those ideas and concepts into an overall framework that provides a very basic blueprint by which middle managers apply these principles.

A highly experienced manager once voiced this maxim to me as we struggled with how to present data in an upcoming executive briefing: "All models are wrong, but some are useful." He went on to explain that all models are somewhat simplistic by their very nature, but should not be dismissed as they may still provide value if applied appropriately. Chapter Six presents one decision support model applicable to all managers, regardless of influence, job scope, employee numbers, industry, or organization type. Pulling all of the concepts outlined in this book together into a single model is an ambitious objective to be sure, but fully attainable.

Figure 8-1 provides a framework that highlights the complex world of leadership decision-making for middle managers. This sandbox is where the middle manager plays every day using the

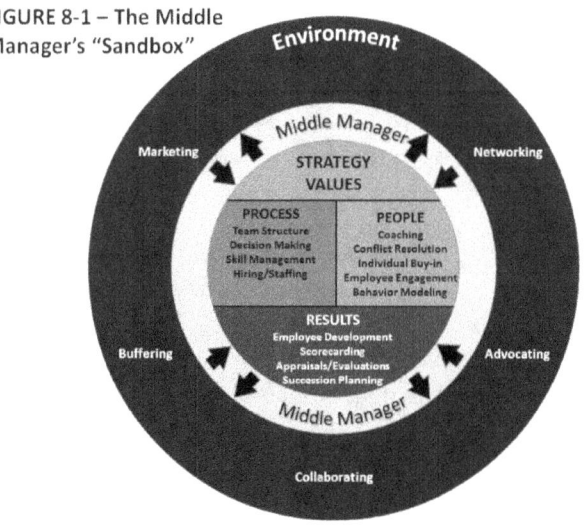

FIGURE 8-1 – The Middle Manager's "Sandbox"

buckets, shovels, and toys at her or his command. Daily decision-making revolves around establishing the right processes to allow the right team with the right skills to focus on the one and only tangible indicator of team effectiveness–results.

While the Sandbox Model highlights specific actions available to managers, it does not include all possible tools to accomplish those actions by any means. Details on how to perform each segment of this model are published in literally thousands of books, articles, seminars and academic programs. The model simplifies and clarifies the many areas of middle management decision-making to provide a broad, high-level tool for all types of managers. The Process, People, and Results sections contain more specific impact areas to implement a solid business plan.

Strategy and Values

The innermost circle of the diagram above highlights the internal aspects of team management. An incoming middle manager frequently inherits Process, People, and past Results, but may alter each of those areas to match the Strategy and Values she or he develops. By necessity, Strategy and Values will evolve over time with changing executive directives, industry pressures, or changing business conditions. After determining how best to support the overall  organizational strategy, the leader crafts and communicates specific values to establish direction and serve as a foundation for their employees' daily decision-making. Direction and decisions for Process and People are made from established Strategy and

Values. Process and People are how strategy becomes reality and results in successful outcomes.

Process

The Process phase is the "machinery" underlying every activity performed by the workgroup. I compare it to machinery because each of these areas requires a lot of thought and consideration to implement, but afterward requires only periodic "maintenance." As an undergraduate college student, I worked at one of the local steel mills in the Dallas/Fort Worth area. The mill ran three shifts around-the-clock for fifty weeks of the year. Every piece of machinery in that mill performed its function as designed and guided by the people operating them. During those fifty active weeks each year, the only downtime allowed was for the repairs and maintenance needed to keep the mill producing steel. However, the entire facility dedicated two weeks each year to what was referred to as "shutdown." During shutdown, the entire mill stopped all operations except the shipping of stockpiled inventory. This two-week period is when the machinists, millwrights, and contractors would overhaul, upgrade, or replace equipment. The objective of this time was not only to repair and replace the equipment needed to keep the mill running as before, but included changes, enhancements and training to improve the mill's performance to meet anticipated future demands.

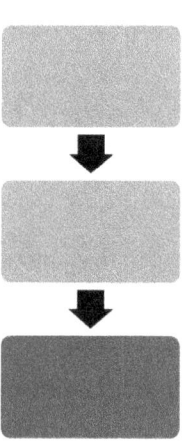

Like the steel mill, every workgroup should have at least a semiannual evaluation and planning time to evaluate the process "machinery" and answer these questions:

- Do the current processes contribute effectively to realizing the group's success criteria?
- Does the decision-making process operate at the speed needed to meet daily requirements and changing business demands?
- Do team members have the skills required by desired processes?

People

In stark contrast to Process, the People block requires continual monitoring, evaluation, and personal investment from the manager. As organizational strategies and values change, so do the demands on employees. Change programs require coaching to build or enhance employee skills, conflict resolution to manage resistance to change, and frequent one-on-one sessions to build and maintain employee buy-in and commitment. Finally, every manager must consistently model the behaviors demanded from others affected by the demands of change. This dedication to demonstrating change behavior is a hugely effective investment into the potential long-term success and perceived leadership.

> Every manager must consistently model behaviors demanded from others.

There are many potential tools and methods to manage people. Every manager has her or his own style, and specific circumstances require differing managerial responses. However, there are several common practices that make the transition period much more meaningful and enjoyable for all when modeled by those managers sponsoring and driving change.

Invest in Vision

Employees of all ages and generations, from Baby Boomers to Millennials, value work that lets them contribute and make a difference. The need for value and purpose cannot always be satisfied with typical offerings like bonuses, stock options, or raises. The most valuable contribution a manager can make to her or his team is vision. A manager who can articulate a clear purpose with a clear direction, and combine that with realistic high expectations, creates the perfect environment for the highest levels of performance.

There are many examples of leaders who have mastered this skill, but one of my favorite examples is Pete Carroll, the Super Bowl-winning coach of an American professional football team, the Seattle Seahawks. Coach Carroll has an established method to build and implement a collaborative, shared vision with each of his assistant coaches. Before training camp begins, he begins each season with a one-on-one meeting with each assistant coach. The meeting begins with Coach Carroll asking the assistant, "What is your vision for this year?" In individual ways, each assistant then outlines what was learned from the previous season, how to implement those lessons into the coming year, and their personal vision for the months ahead. Coach Carroll then spends the next period of time laying out his vision for the team, the organization, and where he sees that assistant participating in that vision. He then outlines the specific contributions he is relying on from that assistant coach to ensure the Seahawks have the best possible chance of winning another championship. Coach Carroll's view for the future is concise, and his expectations and confidence are unwavering during the following discussions and collaborations with his coaches. When the discussion is over, the assistant leaves the room with a clear call to action, knowledge of what is expected, and confidence in his value to the entire team. We would all appreciate our managers making this type of investment into our workplaces and our lives.

Don't Manage a Team, Manage the People

As the turbulence and stress of our work environment increases, it is easy to focus on the team only as a unit and concentrate solely on results. During these times, managers may lose sight of their team as unique individuals with differing passions, interests, life situations, and work styles. However, it is in these times of stress that managers should customize frequent interactions with employees. Be available for one-on-one conversations and deliver lessons for individual developmental opportunities as you are involved in the activity. Do not wait until the project or initiative is complete to provide feedback. It diminishes learning when guidance is given after the chance to apply feedback has passed, and is highly discouraging to the employee. Why not gain immediate value from the feedback instead of having to wait for another opportunity?

Finally, when evaluating people for potential advancement or promotion, don't rely only on the standard, frequently inflexible competency models provided by human resources departments. Generic evaluation and promotion checklists overlook many sources of truly innovative skills and talent among employees who do not fit the standard. Look past organizational barriers for growth opportunities tailored to the ambitions, skills, abilities and experiences of each person. Can we truly expect an innovative and inventive mindset from managers promoted because of how well they fit the standard way of doing things? The answer is obviously "no," but we continue the practice anyway. It is time to change.

As an extension of leading individuals versus a unit, managers and leaders accomplish more by accentuating and investing in the positive attributes of team members rather than focusing on their weaknesses. When we discussed change management in Chapter Seven, we emphasized that people change when they want to change. It is natural for people to be more comfortable, confident, and capable when operating from their strengths. Successful managers find ways to most effectively apply their team members' current strengths and skills. This does not mean that they ignore negative or unproductive behaviors, but they make a very calculated, considered investment in those areas generating the greatest value. When addressing areas of improvement, focus on that which is unacceptable and invest most heavily into bringing forward team strengths.

Make Feedback a Priority

A 2013 study conducted by the Society for Human Resource Management found that only 2% of the managers surveyed provided ongoing feedback to their employees. Did you catch that number? *Only 2%!* Many respondents to the survey relied solely on the frequently despised "performance review". When the only feedback mechanism for a direct report is included with discussion of a raise, bonus, etc. (or lack thereof), the opportunity for open discussion, active listening, and overall impact of the feedback is greatly diminished, if not completely nonexistent. Performance feedback  and planning should be separated from reward discussions for greater effectiveness, and should be conducted much more often. A monthly meeting with each employee for performance feedback and career planning can be a great tool for both manager and employee. The manager can ensure each employee's activities are focused on areas of highest value, and the employee can verify their personal contributions and value to the team on a recurring basis. This removes another risk many managers encounter with their employees: surprises in the performance review. It is my belief that surprises in a performance review are a failure of the manager. An involved manager with a proper feedback process prevents unpleasant surprises of this sort.

This emphasis on providing feedback goes beyond the manager and her or his direct reports. Many times, when a high-performing team succeeds, the manager of that team doesn't believe their contributions are appropriately recognized. If this is a thought process you have experienced or are experiencing, resist the temptation to "blow your own horn" or focus solely on your own accomplishments. Find the glory of your team's success and focus on publicizing your team's capabilities and achievements. Those who lead people will understand a manager's investment into the team's success. Also, when your team encounters difficulty, be the first to accept responsibility. This adds tremendous credibility with those above you in the organization as well as with your team, even if it is an unpleasant task at times.

A last thought on the topic of feedback—utilize this principle with your own career. If you aren't having regularly scheduled feedback meetings with your manager, schedule those meetings on your manager's calendar and initiate those discussions. Receiving feedback can only help ensure your activities are providing tangible impact and value in your boss' perception and judgment.

Listen

Many managerial studies report that employees are happiest and more engaged with their work when they feel free to contribute new ideas and take initiative. Gallup, Inc. (www.gallup.com) has conducted numerous studies and consulting engagements around the world focused on evaluating and increasing employee engagement. In 2016, Gallup reported that only 32% of U.S. employees are "engaged,"—meaning they are involved in, enthusiastic about, and committed to their work and workplace.

Most managers claim to want a team that feels the freedom to openly contribute opinions and take calculated risks. So why don't more workgroups demonstrate those freedoms? Many times, the culprit is the manager promoting their own philosophies or views too strongly. The natural response of many employees in this circumstance is, "Why take risks challenging the current direction when the boss is obviously invested in their opinion?"

The best managers prevent this situation by spending a lot of time listening. They pose challenges and opportunities, ask questions to bring forth opinions, and enlist all resources available to generate solutions and build a vision for success. Perhaps most important of all, they reward innovation and initiative even when it isn't successful, and encourage everyone around them to do the same.

Demonstrate Commitment to Your People

This may be the most difficult principle for middle managers to employ, as it may involve perceived personal risk. Personal security is a key component of many employees' personality profiles. We cannot issue a call for employees to take targeted, calculated risks if we are not willing to support them through both success and failure  when taking those risks. There are many ways managers can demonstrate commitment to good employees without endangering their own well-being, however.

Let me give you an example. I was consulting with a global technology company during a time when hundreds of people lost their jobs through unannounced layoffs. In most cases, the direct managers of the affected employees were not consulted in the decisions of who would stay and who would go, making the unannounced reductions as much a surprise to the managers as to the actual employees.

Most of those who lost their jobs were given the option of immediate separation from the company with severance, or investing a portion of their severance into a sixty-day "grace period" to find another position within the company. No direct assistance was provided to relocate those affected employees within the company—finding another position was entirely up to the individual. As you may guess, the stress levels among those affected was tremendous.

Amid this incredible unrest, one manager demonstrated tremendous leadership and commitment to the people of the organization, even those she may not have met. During her career with the firm, "Christi" had frequently shown herself to be a caring manager and highly competent in team building and vision casting. In her first team meeting following the layoff announcements, "Christi" opened the meeting with a discussion of the current positions open within her team and a declaration that no current team member was eligible for the open positions. She was giving hiring priority to those who had been affected by the layoffs and "not waste proven talent by letting it go outside the company."

Although her investment directly impacted only one position and one individual of the hundreds who had lost their jobs, the impact on her team and everyone they told about the event was nearly immeasurable. Her reputation as a manager who is committed to people was reinforced and high-performing proven candidates will be lined up in the years that follow for a chance to work with her.

This story leads to my final segment on people – if you are a newer manager or have recently accepted a management position, rely on your ability to provide support and not doing the work yourself. One of the most difficult transitions in my managerial career was making the transition from individual contributor to people manager. Many organizations still believe that those who perform the technical functions of the group well should

> Leadership value is enabling others, not doing the work yourself.

be able to lead others well. Unfortunately, many managers simply cannot separate their personal ability to do the job from the necessity to develop others. Teaching others to expand their skills and capabilities requires a different mental focus and is much more important to employees. How do you recognize when a team is limited by their manager? Examine the team members and their performance. If no individual team members can perform the technical aspects of their position better than the manager, learning and innovation has been stunted. The best managers create an environment where employee and team performance increases continually over time.

Results

Between the periodic maintenance of the Process machinery and the continual nurturing of the People, lies the management of Results. Almost all management positions have pre-existing scorecards, metrics, and appraisal systems, but an effective manager must determine how Process and People can most effectively contribute to getting Results. For every metric on the team performance dashboard, exactly how do the group's Processes and People contribute to meeting those goals? Does your current team have the collective skills and abilities to most effectively contribute to those targets? Perhaps most importantly of all, do the existing appraisal and reward systems allow you to recognize and tangibly reward those employees most effectively supporting your Strategy and Values? Employees will always focus their attention and activity on what they are recognized, rewarded, and paid for.

As a last word on Results, if your group is not meeting the assigned goals and metrics, try applying these questions to determine why:

1. Do our team's efforts directly influence the assigned goals or metrics? If not, what can I change to align them?
2. Are we pursuing the appropriate group strategy to attain the desired results?
3. Do we have the right skills in our group to do what we need to do?

4. Do we have effective and efficient processes in place to attain results with the minimum investment of resources (time, people, effort)?
5. Do we have process dependencies on another group that is hindering our efforts?

As stated before, do not fall into the trap of believing that working the same way as before will product different results today and in the future. Working harder, faster, or longer can produce short-term gains, but those gains are not sustainable over time. Production and performance will soon begin to slip once the frenzied "fire drill" activity slows.

Environment

Environment is the most neglected yet potentially most beneficial activity into which a middle manager can invest thought and time. The Environment occurs outside the "four walls" of a manager's specific area of direct authority. A manager contributes huge value to their direct reports with the active and continual monitoring of how the team interacts with other groups within the organization. Many business units and employees have suffered negative work events (also known as layoffs, divestitures, etc.) simply because they had become irrelevant or ineffective and did not realize it. These interactions 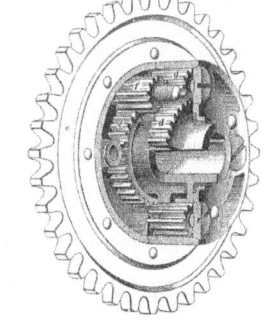 with peer groups are a manager's opportunity to highlight the value the group provides to the organization, and should be frequent and intentional. It is much, much easier to maintain value messaging than regain it once lost or diluted.

We can now break down the Environment segment of the Middle Management Sandbox into its core components.

Marketing: Why should a manager spend precious time and energy on marketing? Decision-makers and key influencers outside of your group cannot always see the value created by your scorecard. Unless these key people receive direct value from the efforts of your workgroup, they typically have little idea of your group's accomplishments. If you are managing a shop floor, a platoon, or a landscaping firm, continually marketing your value contribution is a solid practice.

A marketing plan for your group begins with understanding your team's inputs and outputs. What does your group require from others to perform their functions? What does your group produce that is required for other groups to function? Are those other groups' requirements changing? Are your team's requirements of those groups changing? Many corporate teams become obsolete merely by not providing the outputs needed by other groups. I frequently tell my students, "You can make the highest quality buggy whip in the world for the lowest cost, but in a world of automobiles, it just does not matter. There is no need for them."

The buggy whip analogy is why all managers need to understand and embrace the overall organizational strategy. A successful manager understands not only the inputs and outputs needed for today's desired results, but also grasps how to recognize and respond to upcoming changes. The manager then possesses the ability to demonstrate both how their group has been successful and how their group's contributions directly contributed to the success of other groups.

Buffering: I believe this to be the most underappreciated quality of a great manager. There are many times in any leader's career where they must protect their group from potentially disruptive or distracting initiatives pushed from other parts of the organization, because corporate orders are passed down that may create a great deal of disruption and distraction without contributing to strategic value. It is the role of the manager to make that judgment and shelter the team from those disruptions when possible. This holds true for all levels of leadership, from the CEO down to the third-shift supervisor.

In Summary

 Middle management is where strategy and values are applied through processes and people to produce results.

 Processes are like machinery—we need to inspect, maintain, and overhaul them on a periodic basis.

 For newer and experienced managers, single-minded focus on only your area of control is a common trap. Invest time in:
- *"Building the brand" of your team*
- *Managing others' perception of your team, your people, and the impact to the overall organization*
- *Buffering your team from outside influences that may negatively impact effectiveness and results*

CHAPTER NINE

FROM MIDDLE MANAGEMENT TO... WHAT?

"Everything flows and nothing abides, everything gives way and nothing stays fixed."
~Heraclitus, Greek Philosopher

Asking middle managers to change responsibilities and how they work may seem like trying to teach a fish to tap dance. At the very least, we are asking a person who has reached a high level of personal achievement to change what made them successful. The transition will not come easily. Each person will struggle with potential perceived loss of status, organizational rank, and privilege. At the same time, these individuals will embark on a new learning curve and embrace a new career path where personal impact is not defined by an organizational chart, but rather by influence and creativity. Evaluating the psychological effects of these changes should be included in the change planning.

When mapping out the next steps for current middle managers, it is critical to remember the value these resources provide for organizations. Middle managers frequently possess a decade or more of direct experience in the company, high achievement records (hence their management role), knowledge of customers and suppliers, knowledge of how things get done, and how many basic processes may be improved.

There are many alternate positions for these valuable resources, but we will focus on these specific roles:
- Program Manager
- Change Manager
- Coach
- Alliance Manager/Strategic Relations Manager

Middle Manager to Program Manager

This transition may be the most straightforward, once the terminology involved is out of the way. First, program managers are *not* project managers. A project manager oversees the resources, tasks, timelines, and communications associated with a specific project or projects. In contrast, program management is a business support function that coordinates groups of related projects to ensure all initiatives contribute to business objectives and produce the desired benefits to the organization.

Let's use a shipbuilding analogy to demonstrate the differences. Suppose a Viking village wanted to launch an expedition to the New World to bring back materials needed by the villagers. To support this initiative (or "program"), a ship would be needed to transport the captain and crew to their intended destination. Let's build a ship! In such an endeavor, a project manager for the shipbuilding activities (or "project") would:

- ensure the hiring of enough workers with appropriate skills
- schedule shifts for the workers to perform their functions at the appropriate phase of ship completion
- acquire materials needed and have them delivered to the build site when required
- communicate continually with the crew managers to make sure they have what's needed when it is needed
- address any variances that may impact getting the ship built on time, on budget and according to specifications

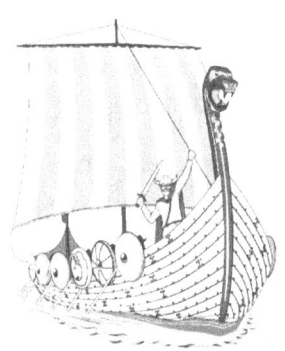

Once the ship is constructed, inspections are completed, and the builders are paid, the project manager's responsibility in this story is complete. The project is complete—we have a ship! However, the overall outcomes desired by the village are not yet achieved. Much work remains to realize the desired result of launching a successful expedition to the New World!

While the tremendously competent project manager directs shipbuilding, here are a few other projects underway, including:

- selection of expedition leaders
- clarification of the direction, distance, and specific results expected from the overall expedition
- definition of what skills are needed by those who will sail the ship
- creating and communicating the need for sailors to the surrounding villages
- acquiring the sailing crew
- evaluating the crew's skills, identifying training needs, creating and implementing a training regimen for the new crew
- coordinating crew readiness with the ship readiness

As you can see, even in this fictitious example, there are many projects (shipbuilding, recruiting/training, cross-project coordination, and communications) included in the overall program. The summary difference between project and program management is this—the program manager can perform every aspect of the duties listed above to perfection, meet all timelines, hire and train all of the needed people, and still not perform his or her function successfully! Why? Simple—the contribution the overall program makes toward the desired results determines success or failure. Success is only achieved when the ship completes a journey to the New World and returns with supplies needed by the village. The combined whole of process, people, and business results is the primary differentiator between project and program management.

Middle managers frequently fill the program management role in a highly effective manner due to previous focus on business results. Program managers who move into the role from a successful middle management position have direct, practical knowledge of how to focus time, energy, and people on attaining demonstrable outcomes. These same principles translate directly into the planning, communications, training, and coaching needed to guide multiple workgroups along a coordinated path to business goals.

Middle Manager to Change Manager

When reading the portions of Chapter Seven dealing with change management, you may have realized the relationship between daily management activities and the people-oriented aspects of managing change. Middle managers are the most important contributors to successful organizational change. Any significant transformation project depends on the concept of "critical mass." The *Merriam-Webster Dictionary* defines critical mass as, "A size, number, or amount large enough to produce a particular result." Sustainable change occurs when enough individuals accept, implement, and actively support the behaviors required by the change. This includes the skills outlined in Chapter Two, where we discussed

how to break down overall organizational strategy into daily business plans and workgroup policies.

A huge additional benefit of having former managers in the change management role is their familiarity with the company culture, change history, key stakeholders, and influencers within the organization. This is an invaluable aid in creating and communicating what may be the most important content of a change directive—what is frequently referred to as the WIIFM (what's in it for me?) message. A thorough understanding of the relationship between strategy and daily activity allows a former middle manager deep insight for establishing the need to change. If leaders do not answer the question "why should I change?" or the message is unclear, infrequent, and not reinforced from multiple sources, failure is the common result. Various learning research suggests a person needs to hear a specific message at least seven times for the message to "stick." This need to repeat is why we must endure the endlessly repeated advertisements during special events broadcasted on television.

Change programs benefit tremendously from a former middle manager who understands influence without authority, which executives are best recruited for target audiences, and how to reinforce messages over time to create the highest potential for successful change.

Middle Manager to Coach

Transformational change on a corporate level is difficult, costly, and time-consuming. Becoming a learning organization, implementing LEAN manufacturing, or undergoing a large reorganization requires employees to enhance skills while altering their thinking and behavior. Most affected employees will require mentoring, coaching, and guidance to build those new skills. Fortunately, the role of middle manager encompasses those exact abilities, and former managers can make very effective coaches and mentors.

While the transition from middle manager to coach usually requires some retooling, teaching skills are readily taught. Even if training in basic instructional skills is required, it is a small investment compared to the hiring of external personnel to perform the  same function. An external instructor will never possess the knowledge of the culture, processes, personalities, and stakeholders of the organization that a veteran employee possesses as second nature due to years of experience.

Not every middle manager can make the transition to coach and teacher successfully, however. Some will consider such a role beneath their dignity or capability. Some will simply lack the necessary interpersonal skills, charisma, or communication ability. Others will believe better opportunities exist elsewhere outside of their current organization. For those who accept the challenge, develop the needed skills, and focus on the people, their value is frequently priceless.

Middle Manager to Relationship or Alliance Manager

Most large organizations in today's global economy depend on a partnership structure for some part of their business model. For instance, Microsoft does not directly sell much of their software—many, many sales are led by a network of partners. IBM also has a huge network of business partners to help them meet the demand for services across the globe. Our economy is one of partnerships that create a chain of suppliers, service providers, vendors, and end customers.

Most organizations today are either creating or enhancing their ability to meet ever-increasing customer and business demands. A key part of that process is the effective development and management of partner relationships. Common strategic relationship management activities may include:

- certifying and auditing key suppliers
- evaluating key delivery partners and enhancing their capabilities to market and deliver to end customers
- working with suppliers and vendors to create, enhance and manage just-in-time (JIT) manufacturing functions
- identifying and developing marketing and sales divisions within new markets
- managing research and talent acquisition programs with universities or other firms

These activities are a natural extension of most organizations' value creation processes. The effective management of these partner resources is the key to harnessing the best possible application of available knowledge from both external and internal talent.

What is the bottom-line value of utilizing the skills, experiences, and abilities of middle managers in these partner alliance roles? Repurposing middle managers into these roles reinvests the skills and experience already possessed by current employees. Staffing and training costs are reduced or eliminated entirely. The executive team also sends a very positive message throughout the organization by highlighting the value of current employees while making needed changes to address an uncertain future.

In Summary

 Middle management experience builds skills and abilities easily transferable to functions that are not a direct promotion to the next managerial level.

 Changing from a managerial role to an individual contributor role is difficult for many, but may yield great personal satisfaction.

 Potential alternate roles for middle managers are program manager, change manager, coach/trainer or relationship manager.

CHAPTER TEN

CROSSING THE FINISH LINE

"Past success secures future failure if we continue to bask in its glow for too long"
~Faisal Ghosa, M.D.

WE now reach the final chapter, but I must first apologize for the misleading chapter title. The activities outlined in this book are a never-ending process for middle managers. Today's organizational demands require frequent identification of threats and opportunities with appropriate planned responses. There is no finish line to this cycle as a middle manager, executive, individual contributor, or independent contractor.

Not all is a world of doom and gloom, however. I am a huge believer in "cheat sheets" or "cube notes.". All material in this book sums up with "A-B-C." Chapters One and Two encourage us to Align ourselves and our teams with overall organizational strategy, values, and direction. Chapter Three through Chapter Seven highlight how to **B**uild your operations (people and processes) to align with the capabilities required by your organizational strategy and business plan. Chapters Eight and Nine highlight the requirement to **C**omplete your strategies and tactics so your organizational group provides the output needed by your managers, your peers, and your customers.

Every activity conducted by successful middle managers falls

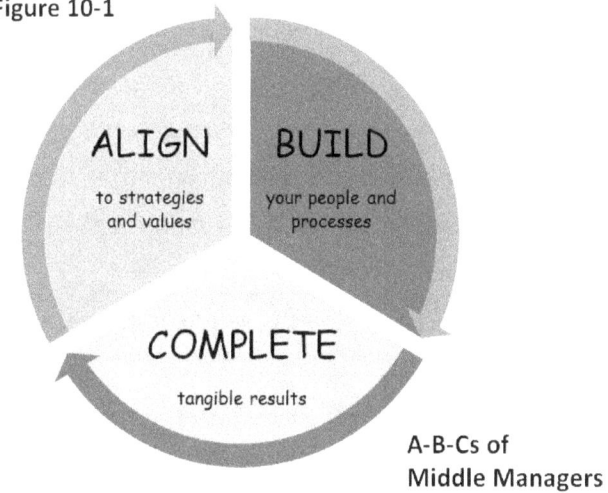

Figure 10-1

A-B-Cs of Middle Managers

within these categories. Every business course, organizational skills training, and human resources enrichment program fits within this structure. Figure 10-1 puts the entire "survive and thrive" mentality into a straightforward format.

The tremendous pressures on today's managers are not from demands on personal skills, techniques, or technical knowledge. Employees throughout time have been required to improve skills and abilities as their career progresses. The pressure results from the continuous attack on the leaders' mental model of how to manage effectively in highly turbulent environments. Following the framework demonstrated in this book will allow leaders to operate in any industry, any organization, and any organizational structure whether for-profit, nonprofit, public service, volunteer, or self-employed. The key is to understand the strategic system. When there is an understanding of the system and how the parts of that system interact, managers better understand how to contribute and support effectively.

> *"Managers are not confronted with problems that are independent of each other, but with dynamic situations that consist of complex systems of changing problems that interact with each other. I call such situations messes... Managers do not solve problems, they manage messes."*
>
> ~Russell Ackoff, Operations Theorist

IN CLOSING

I would love to hear your feedback on the content of this book, whether positive, negative, or neutral. Please let me know how I can enhance this book, follow up with another book, or develop a speaking series.

Most of all, let me know how to better help the most under-appreciated segment of our companies, communities, and military—those who manage in the middle—the "bulls in the ring."

NOTES

ABOUT THE AUTHOR

M. Shane Putman is a veteran consultant and university business instructor. His former clients and employers have included Microsoft, Hewlett-Packard, IBM, JC Penney, Bally's Corporation and Electronic Data Systems. He is a frequent conference speaker and business strategy facilitator. His academic credentials include an MBA in Strategic Management and current pursuit of a PhD in Organizational Leadership.

www.ingramcontent.com/pod-product-compliance
Lightning Source LLC
Chambersburg PA
CBHW050112230526
45470CB00004B/1797